BANNACK
A Growing Up Story In The Vigilante West

BANNACK

A Growing Up Story In The Vigilante West

JERRY DELANEY

ReadersMagnet, LLC

Bannack: A Growing Up Story In The Vigilante West
Copyright © 2020 by Jerry Delaney

Published in the United States of America
ISBN Paperback: 978-1-951775-92-6
ISBN eBook: 978-1-951775-93-3

All rights reserved. No part of this publication may be reproduced, stored in a retrieval system or transmitted in any way by any means, electronic, mechanical, photocopy, recording or otherwise without the prior permission of the author except as provided by USA copyright law.

The opinions expressed by the author are not necessarily those of ReadersMagnet, LLC.

ReadersMagnet, LLC
10620 Treena Street, Suite 230 | San Diego, California, 92131 USA
1.619.354.2643 | www.readersmagnet.com

Book design copyright © 2020 by ReadersMagnet, LLC. All rights reserved.
Cover design by Ericka Obando
Interior design by Shemaryl Tampus

Contents

Acknowledgments 7

PART ONE: JOURNEY TO THE GOLD FIELDS

Chapter One 11
Chapter Two 17
Chapter Three 22
Chapter Four 28
Chapter Five 33
Chapter Six 39
Chapter Seven 41
Chapter Eight 48
Chapter Nine 54
Chapter Ten 58
Chapter Eleven 65
Chapter Twelve 68
Chapter Thirteen 74
Chapter Fourteen 79
Chapter Fifteen 86

PART II: BANNACK

Chapter Sixteen 99
Chapter Seventeen 104
Chapter Eighteen 106
Chapter Nineteen 111
Chapter Twenty 114
Chapter Twenty-One 119
Chapter Twenty-Two 122
Chapter Twenty-Three 126
Chapter Twenty-Four 132
Chapter Twenty-Five 136
Chapter Twenty-Six 140
Chapter Twenty-Seven 144
Chapter Twenty-Eight 149
Chapter Twenty-Nine 153
Chapter Thirty 156
Chapter Thirty-One 160
Chapter Thirty-Two 163
Chapter Thirty-Three 169
Chapter Thirty-Four 175
Chapter Thirty-Five 179
Chapter Thirty-Six 182
Chapter Thirty-Seven 188
Chapter Thirty-Eight 192
Chapter Thirty-Nine 195
Chapter Forty 199
Chapter Forty-One 202
Chapter Forty-Two 207

Epilogue 211
Afterword 215

Acknowledgments

My respect and thanks to the authors of *Hanging the Sheriff*, by F. E. Boswell and R. E. Mather, for their pioneering historical research into the whole story of Henry Plummer and the Montana Vigilantes.

As a boy growing up in Montana, I had been taught in public school that Henry Plummer was the most notorious outlaw in the state's history. With their contemporary research, Boswell and Mather eradicated all doubt in my mind that the historical record was demonstrably wrong.

I would also like to acknowledge the work of Frederick Allen whose recent book, *A Decent Orderly Hanging*, is a thoughtful, well-written, and conscientiously researched account of the period. However, in my opinion, Allen does not pursue the implications of his own research to their logical conclusion, which is to say there is not a shred of credible evidence that Henry Plummer was guilty of the crimes charged him by the vigilantes.

Authors of books that contain the official story—e.g., Thomas J. Dimsdale, *The Vigilantes of Montana*; Nathaniel Pitt Langford, *Vigilante Days and Ways*; Lew L. Calloway, *Montana's Righteous Hangmen*; Edwin Ruthven, *Purple, The Perilous Trail*—confirm the observation that history is fatally infected by the character and prejudices of those who write it.

PART ONE

JOURNEY TO THE GOLD FIELDS

Chapter One

"YOU BEEN STEALIN MY WHISKEY!" Those were the first words Pa spoke that night. We were standing out in the barn, and it was pitch dark except for a spray of light from a kerosene lamp nearby. The barn door was closed because I'd shut it behind me when I came in.

"Well, what ya got to say for yerself?"

I looked down and kicked a few scraps of old hay to one side with my boot. Trouble was, I didn't have a damn thing to say for myself. About a month earlier I'd found where he kept his whiskey bottle hidden in the barn and took my first taste. Nearly made me puke. My whole body shuddered like I'd touched electricity, so I swore I'd never do that again. But after a week or so passed, I got an itch to feel that electric shock a second time. So I took another taste and gagged just like the first time and wondered how a man could take a big gulp of the stuff. Then I did something really stupid. I went back to feel the electric shock again and spilled some of the whiskey on the floor.

"I marked the label with my thumbnail," Pa shouted. "That's how I know."

He knew, all right. Well, I reckoned there was hell to pay for admitting it, but I wasn't about to lie either. "You're right Pa."

He glared at me a full minute, I bet, not saying a word. He was a tall, thin man with a face like a piece of outcrop, and when his jaw was set and his eyes fixed, he could make a rock sweat. On top of that, while he was staring at me, I could smell whiskey on his breath, a full five paces away.

The old man turned quick and walked over to where he kept the switch he used for discipline on me and my four sisters, although mostly me. Last thing I wanted to see was that god-awful switch again. He always cut a thick branch from the willow tree in our backyard, and it cracked across your ass like a leather whip.

"Grab your ankles, Billy."

I still can't say why I bridled that particular night. Seemed like I'd grabbed my ankles a hundred times before, and it'd never crossed my mind to buck his authority. But that night something stirred in me. All I could think was *No, goddamit, no more.*

Maybe it was because I got fed up with him saying one thing and doing another. As a strict Presbyterian he'd give a fiery sermon on the evils of liquor and then go out to the barn and drink himself senseless. To me that amounted to talking out of both sides. Then, too, I was turning sixteen and had grown a lot taller in the past year, right up close to his six feet, and even though I was skinny as a reed, folks said I was all gristle and nearly as strong as he was.

Anyway, I looked at him real hard and said, "You're not gonna do that no more, Pa." When I said that, I felt a surge of pride rise in me as if a brass band had just started playing "The Battle Cry of Freedom."

His eyes widened, and he dropped the switch and hauled off and slapped me hard as he could across the face. The blow almost knocked me down, but I kept my balance and stood there glaring at him, my face burning hot. 'Course, that slap stopped the band playing mighty quick. Still, I glared back and then, without thinking, hauled off and slapped him just as hard. He stood his ground, his mouth so tight his teeth showed. He slapped me, and I slapped him, and then we did it again, quick-like.

My face was burning like a bonfire, but I wasn't about to back down. Now, lucky for me I saw it coming, the way he pulled back his shoulder and arm, because I dodged to one side just as his fist went firing by my face. Crazy mad, he lunged at me with both hands open, tryin to get his fingers around my neck, but I grabbed him, and we fell to the barn floor and started rolling and flailing and kicking at each other in a fury I've never experienced before or since.

Somehow I managed to kick him away with one foot and got out of his grasp, jumped to my feet, and ran to the back of the barn where it was dark, and there I hid behind our Sunday buggy. I didn't want to fight anyway. This was crazy.

He got the kerosene lamp from the shelf, held it up with one hand, and started back toward me and the buggy, the white light advancing with him into the darkness where I hid. The two work horses started snorting and stamping in their stalls as if they smelled the sweat and blood and anger in the air. That was the only sound for a moment there, those horses snorting and stamping.

Then my mouth about dropped open when Pa grabbed a pitchfork leaning against the wall and headed straight toward me, lamp in one hand, pitchfork in the other. He put the kerosene lamp on the buggy seat so it cast a tent of light over the two of us standing on opposite sides of the buggy. Watching him peer at me with his hand raised, ready to strike, I couldn't hardly believe my eyes. I was so stupefied, I forgot about being scared. He'd been mean before but never like this.

"Put that down, Pa, you dont know what you're doin!"

He started around the buggy after me, and I slid to the other side, keeping the buggy between us. "Look, Pa," I said, "you dont want to do this. Think about Mama, forget about me."

He still had that crazed look in his eyes, but those words stopped him. He stood up and, after a long, silent moment, dropped the pitchfork to the floor. Looking at me in the light of the kerosene lamp, his face seemed to go limp.

"Listen to me, Billy!" His words rang out in the hollow of the barn. "I'm goin back to the house to bed, and if I get up tomorrow morning and you're still around, I'll make your life so damn miserable, you'll wish I'd done killed you." He took a breath and said softer, "You never listened to a damn thing I told you anyways."

I let the air out with a real sigh of relief. I groped around and found a bale of hay and sat down. Maybe he was right about that, me not listening to what he said, but he was always talking about God and saying the main reason for living was to get ready for dying so you "don't get throwed in the flames of hell." I just didn't take to it.

My mother once said, "Billy, your father has some fixed ideas about how you're supposed to behave in life, and you got different ones. You're stakin out a hard row to hoe."

Those words stuck like a burr in my mind. As I sat there in the darkness of that barn, I told myself I didn't care if I was staking out a hard row; from now on I was staking one out.

I tasted some blood in my mouth and spit it on the floor. My face burned, and one eye was hurting, but I felt nothing but relief. I said out loud, "All right, Pa. If that's the way you want it, I'll goddamn go. All we do is fight anyhow."

———⋄※⋄———

My mama and sisters were in bed, thank God, so I went quietly to my room at the back of the house on the second floor and started packing. Since it was spring and still cold at night, I reckoned I ought to take my wool sweater and black overcoat. I stuffed my favorite trousers, the homemade ones colored brown in butternut oil by Mama, plus two shirts and socks and hankies in my knapsack, fetched my toothbrush, then wrapped up a brown army blanket to carry separately and tied it on top of the knapsack. I scraped up all the money I'd saved, which amounted to about five dollars. Finally, I lay down on the bed to let things sink in.

It was Mama I was gonna miss. My sisters, too, but mostly Mama. She had those big brown eyes that looked like she was always holding a losing hand of cards. She wasn't the kind of mama'd hug you good night, but she stuck up for me in my war with the old man, and I loved her for that. 'Course in the end, she had to give in to him and do what she was supposed to do, which said to me that doing what she was supposed to do and what was right weren't the same thing.

There was no doubt where I wanted to go. I'd read in the papers about the new gold discoveries up in the Northwest Territory, and all the stories said an enterprising young man could make a lot of money if he just worked hard enough. Since I lived outside a little town called Ada, not far from Springfield, home of you know who, I figured I'd head south and west to St. Louis, then catch one of those new steamers up the Missouri all the way to the end of the line at Fort Benton. When I got to the gold fields, I'd stake out a few claims and make a fortune.

When it came time to go, when I was sure everyone else was sound asleep, I felt real heavy lying there in the bed, as if I was too heavy to lift myself. I wondered maybe I ought to beg Pa to let me stick around till I was seventeen. But then I said hell no, this was no way to live anyways, slopping hogs, chopping corn, saying yessir, nossir every two minutes. Oliver Twist ran away from home younger'n me, as I recollected. Besides, I kept telling myself, I'd come back someday and see my mama and sisters again, and meantime I'd keep in touch by writing.

I bit down real hard and got up.

After getting into my long-sleeved shirt, overalls, sweater, and black overcoat, which was way too hot, and throwing on my wide-brimmed hat, I tiptoed downstairs to the back door carrying my boots in one hand. 'Course, I ought to have something to eat along the way, so I found a candle, lit it, and went into the pantry, where I poured out a sack of dried navy beans, mixed together another sack of coffee and sugar, grabbed a loaf of bread, picked up a fork and spoon and matches, and stuffed everything in my knapsack. I spilled a few things on the floor and winced a little thinking of Mama cleaning it up the next day.

Then the idea hit me, it'd be a lot easier with some more money. So I went to where Pa cached his savings, pulled his money box from under a floorboard, and counted out 430 dollars and some change. Jesus, was I surprised how much he had. I counted out

125 dollars for myself, my fingers shaking a mite, thinking this was more than enough to book a passage on one of the steamers going to the northwest. I thought about leaving a note promising to pay it back, but I didn't have pencil and paper.

    I blew out the candle and put my boots on again, tiptoed to the back door, and peered out into the cold night air. Seemed like there was no moon or stars; the sky was black as tar. *Well*, I said to myself, *here goes*, and took the first step on my journey to the gold fields.

Chapter Two

EARLIER THAT YEAR MY MAMA had bought a book called *The Oregon Trail* from one of those traveling book salesmen, and after reading it, she handed it to me and said, "Let's see if you're smart enough to read this, Billy." She knew how to bait the hook, all right, always asking if I was smart enough to read something. Anyway, I read the whole Oregon Trail book, and afterward, as usual, she asked, "Well, what have you learned, Billy Mayfair?"

I thought about that awhile and then said, "What the book told me is, a life lived as adventure is better'n a life lived at home doing everyday things." She smiled at that.

So being kicked out of the house didn't bother me. I was gonna leave anyway sooner or later. Pa just made it sooner.

As I said, it was pitch dark that night. I couldn't even see the next-door farm, it was so dark. A couple times, I stumbled in the ruts of the cart path 'cause I couldn't see my boots. I reckoned by noon the next day I'd be at the turnpike, and then after five or six days walking and hitching west, I'd be in St. Louis. Pa said St. Louis was a sink of iniquity where fallen women tempted men with the evil apple of fornication. How's that for another reason to go to St. Louis?

'Course, I was heading closer to the war. That's all everybody talked about, the war and how awful it was. Most people were getting pretty sick of it after two years and sick of Abraham Lincoln too.

Not Pa, though. He used to read about the war out loud from the Springfield newspaper nearly every night at the dinner table. Besides the newspaper, he read us stories from *Harper's Weekly* about how the colored were whipped and beaten like farm animals in the slave states. You can probably guess he was a devout abolitionist. During one stretch he read *Uncle Tom's Cabin* out loud while sitting at the dinner table.

I'd have liked to take a different point of view from Pa, just on principle, but on the subject of slavery, I didn't see any other view to take. No man ought to own another; that was plain common sense.

Truth is, I learned a number of things from all that talk by Pa. I learned that at the beginning of the war there were four million slaves in this country out of a population of thirty-two million people. 'Course, most of them were down south, but quite a few were in the border states too. Over 150,000 of those slaves were in Missouri where I was headed. The peculiar thing about Missouri was, it had both Union and secessionist folks living side by side. The Union army controlled the government of the state, but a bunch of rebels were still fighting a guerrilla war there, and bushwhackers on both sides were slaughtering each other every day. Pa said Missouri was in a state of disunion.

But I wasn't worried. At that moment I had no idea how the war was gonna turn my life upside down and inside out. What I was worried about, as I walked down that dirt cart path on my way to St. Louis, was Pa notifying the sheriff his money'd been stolen. The sheriff would no doubt send out a telegram to all the towns around to watch out for the likes of Billy Mayfair. That was what worried me.

The cart path went on for a couple miles before it narrowed to a trail that cut through the woods. "Damnation, Billy," I said out loud when stepping into the dark woods, "a man don't find adventure staying home all his life." The sound of my voice raised my spirits.

I used to talk out loud to myself on the farm sometimes when nobody was around. I practiced imitating other people so I could make everybody laugh at the dinner table. For instance, I used to imitate my cousin Ernie, who had a stutter so bad that it left everybody leaning forward in suspense to catch the next word. Even Pa sometimes laughed before he caught himself and said it wasn't right making fun of others.

About three o'clock that morning it started to rain, first a little bit, then cats and dogs. Nothing like a cold rain on a dark night to press down the spirits. I scampered over to a stand of oaks alongside the trail and felt around in the dark for a spot under one of the big ones. The oak tree and my wide-brimmed hat sheltered me from the rain, but my overalls were still soaked, and it was cold.

I sat hunched up under that tree, trying to catch a few winks, but too many thoughts kept buzzing through my mind. I thought of my friend Jack Coppedge and wished he was going with me. I had a vision in my mind of slipping over to his farm first thing in the morning before sunup and catching him in the barn milking one of the cows. "C'mon with me, Jack," I'd say, "there's a brand-new life for us in the gold fields, you and me." I knew he wouldn't even look up, though, just stare into the pail of milk. Old Jack'd stay home doing everyday things all his life. But I'd miss him.

And I'd miss a couple of other friends too, including Sara Belnap, who I consorted with at the Saturday night dances. Sara had big, turned-up lips that made me want to clamp mine on them every time I saw her. I did, too, kiss her quite a few times, but that's as far as she'd let me go; never would let me slip my hand under her dress and touch her bare breasts.

"Is that all you boys think about?" she'd say.

And I'd say, "Yep." She didn't know we walked around with a hard-on half the time.

Pretty soon the sky began to pale in the east. "So what you gonna do, Billy?" I asked myself out loud, teeth clacking from the cold. "Let's git!"

After a while the rain abated some but still came down in a light drizzle. The whole countryside looked dripping wet and raw in the drizzly dawn light.

A couple cornfields I passed by were still strewn with broken-down stalks from last year's crop, a reminder that I wouldn't be chopping corn for the hogs this year. Thank God. Seemed to me those fields and old stalks should have been turned under by this time. These long, green fields looked misty in the pale white light of dawn, silent and still, like a picture with nothing in it.

Several other fields I walked by had just been plowed, the broken sod turned into long rows of dark brown earth, real muddy in spots, nothing to walk through. I noticed green sprouts of wheat were popping up in some places and was surprised to see little shoots of corn here and there, even though it seemed awful early for them, this year having been a wet spring and the seeds not planted till late. That corn would be knee high by the Fourth.

Anyway, the land was giving birth to the crops, and it seemed like the crops were ahead of schedule.

I walked steady all morning and did see a few people working in the fields, but nobody seemed to notice me, which was just fine. Just after noon I reached the turnpike heading west to St. Louis, soaked and cold and hungry. *Jesus, where are those griddle cakes, Mama?* I found a spot in a thicket of oak and elm, pulled together some poles and branches, and made myself a dry lean-to. Then I wondered how I was going to make a fire with only wet wood around.

Nearby, a black oak had a dead branch that looked protected from the rain by the higher branches. I shimmied up about fifteen feet and broke it off, then went to work on a fire. With the jackknife my folks had given me for Christmas, I whittled off a pile of shavings, collected some dry twigs below a rock outcrop, and started it going. Once I got the fire lit, I had no trouble building it high and hot. With a fire and my tin cup and some water from a nearby pool, you can guess what I did next—fixed the best cup of coffee ever tasted. I washed down my loaf of bread with it.

A curious woodchuck came by and stared at me while I ate; we looked at each other a few seconds, then he darted off like he had something better to do. I took off my soaked pants and shorts and wrung them out and draped them on sticks next to the fire. I got so warm, standing naked from the waist down facing the fire, that I got a real powerful hard-on that wouldn't go down no matter how many times I told it to. In my mind I saw those turned-up lips of Sara Belnap and couldn't help squeezing a couple times. Then the next thing you know I took a hard grip, and bang, like a pistol I spit right into the fire, just like that, and then watched the stuff sizzle on a burning piece of wood.

I always felt a little ashamed after jacking off, even though I didn't believe the preacher when he said masturbation makes you speak with a stutter and leads to a life of crime. He used to lower his voice and say real solemn to us boys, "Onan, son of Judah, cast his seed on the ground, and the Lord slew him for his sin." I had to smile. What about casting it in the fire? And watching it sizzle on a piece of wood like a fried egg on the griddle? Was I gonna get slain? What about casting it into your hanky? That's what I did most of the time, then washed the hanky out so Mama wouldn't see. What about casting it into Sara Belnap? That was something devoutly to be wished for.

I was a sinner, all right, no doubt, but I couldn't get too worked up about it. All the boys jacked off and sometimes even together, standing in a circle shooting off into the hay, to see who could squirt the farthest. 'Course, that was a few years ago, when I was younger. Now I did it maybe three, four times a week but only as a temporary thing, till I found a woman who'd do the real thing with me. Then no more casting seed anywhere except where it belonged.

That made me think of what Pa said about St. Louis, and I resolved then and there St. Louis was the place where I was going to do the real thing and cast my seed where it belonged.

While I stood there by the fire, letting my things get a little drier, I could see an occasional wagon train passing by in the distance on the turnpike to St. Louis. It crossed my mind that I'd be better off joining a party of immigrants than continuing on by myself. The law would be looking for a lone boy, not some migrant.

So I waited till I saw a caravan coming up the road from afar, and then I jumped into my still wet clothes and took off to join them.

Chapter Three

Those eight wagons were a pretty sight moving down the turnpike at a nice, easy pace. The first seven, pulled by oxen, were easy to recognize as Conestogas because of their high canvas tops, but the last wagon was different. It was a plain old work wagon like the one we used on the farm to cart dirt and manure, piled high with personal belongings covered by a canvas tarp, and pulled by two mules. A man walked ahead of the mules, a tethered cow plodded along behind the wagon, and the family—looked like eight or nine of them—walked along in silence. And then, lucky for me, I sighted a boy about my age.

"Jumpin Jaysus!" he said when I appeared out of the blue beside him. "Where'd you come from?"

"I'm settin out to try my luck in the gold fields," I said. "Mind if I walk along for a spell?"

He spit through his teeth to one side and said, "Not at all, not at all."

His name was Jimmy Plunkett, and he was Irish. "Jaysus, have ye never seen an Irishman before?" was the way he put it. He was about six inches shorter than me and skinny as a rod, his hair shaved off because, I learned later, he'd gotten infected by lice.

Truth was I had never seen an Irish boy before. My pa said the Irish were all papists who took orders from the whore of Rome.

Jimmy said they'd left Ireland thirteen years ago when he was a lad of six, and the family had been living in New York City ever since. They'd gone from being hungry in Ireland to being scared in New York. Right now they were bloody glad to get out of New York before the conscription started.

I'd heard about conscription, that it was coming to Illinois this summer for boys nineteen years old, but since it didn't affect me, I hadn't thought much about it.

Jimmy continued. "My da says he don't want me fightin no war rich Americans are getting outta by payin three hundred dollars. That's a year's wages for him." I was so stupid I didn't know a man could buy his way out of the war for three hundred dollars. Jimmy said, "It's a rich man's war, Billy, and a poor man's fight."

Some folks around our town would've called that kind of talk treasonous, I'm sure, but it didn't bother me.

"We're bound for St. Louis," Jimmy said, "gettin a homestead north along the Mississippi River. You get one free if you work it for five years. Da says the land's so rich, the corn pops up soon as you drop the seeds in the ground."

Pa used to say the only reason the government was giving out free land in the West was because the dirty immigrants from Ireland were ruining the eastern cities. About three million of them were taking away jobs from real Americans. Then every last one of them voting Democrat just like the Pope wanted.

The rest of the Plunkett family snuck glances at me as we walked along, but nobody said anything. My new friend looked to be the oldest in a family of seven children. One of them, a girl about five, seemed mighty young to be walking all the way west. I noticed one fella behind us didn't look much like the others in the family, shuffling along with a goofy look on his face, sometimes slobbering like a baby into a white bib on his chest. I learned later the Plunketts were obliged to take care of him because he was Jimmy's uncle. He reminded me of an idiot I saw once talking to himself outside a feed store in Springfield.

Mr. Plunkett came over, introduced himself, and said I was welcome to walk along with his family as long as I wanted. He wasn't much taller than Jimmy, about five foot six inches, but his face seemed a lot older, a small, milk white face that looked like he hadn't spent much time in the sun. He had a big wide-brimmed hat on that shaded him. Although he was harder to understand than Jimmy because of his thick Irish accent, he was friendly and asked me questions like he was real interested in what I had to say.

Then the mules started getting skittish, so Mr. Plunkett walked over to take charge.

While we were walking along side by side, Jimmy Plunkett coughed up a gob of spit from the back of his mouth and hawked it out in a high arc about twenty-five feet across the road into the ditch. It was a mighty impressive cast of spit, and I told him so.

Presently we heard this thunder of hooves on the road behind us. Two blue-coated men rode by on horseback, shouting, "Get off the road, off to the side with ya!" The wagons and people fell to one side, and pretty soon a whole column of Union troops marched by, carrying rifles on their shoulders, so close I could see they looked fresh and clean in their bright uniforms and funny tilted hats. Seemed like all of them were about my age. I figured they must be new recruits on their way to join the main army in Missouri.

The countryside was hilly along this part of the road, hills rolling out far as you could see, a thick rug of wavy green woods. The turnpike sliced right through the woods, rising up over the smaller hills and swerving around the larger ones. Our whole wagon train slowed when we were on the rise, and then when we started on the downslope, Jimmy jumped up onto the buckboard and used the brake to keep our wagon from running away.

It wasn't raining any longer, thank God, but it looked like it could start again any time. The sky was gray and sunless, and the clouds moved slow and heavy above us. A flock of geese passed overhead so low you could hear their wings thrashing in the air.

A while later we were walking along talking when all of a sudden we heard a bunch of shots popping away in the distance up front of us. Sounded like Fourth of July firecrackers, only far away. They kept popping for about five minutes and then stopped just as suddenly as they started. Then it started to rain again. Damnation.

"Sounds like an ambush up there," Mr. Plunkett said loudly to the whole family.

He was right too. We got to the place in about twenty minutes and found a terrible scene of slaughter and bloodshed. The attack had happened along a stretch of road where the woods bent in so close the attackers could fire nearly point-blank at the passing soldiers. The smell of gunpowder still hung in the air, and men and rifles and knapsacks were scattered over the ground. A lot of soldiers were wounded and bleeding and waiting for help, while others were being patched up on the spot with white bandages. The uniforms that looked so starched clean before were bloody and torn and dirty, hats lying in the mud.

Then, with a shiver, I noticed a pile of dead bodies all tangled up together, lying in the mud and rain.

A soldier stood on the side of the road waving his arms for us to keep moving, but by this time the whole wagon train had stopped, and everyone was staring in silence as if they were stupefied. I noticed the young Irish girls had clapped their hands to their mouths, and the little five-year-old ran to Mrs. Plunkett and jammed her head against her dress.

I took notice of one boy about my age lying out there in the mud, blood all over his face, screaming in pain, and I felt that scream like someone had stuck a knife in my belly. Then I saw Mrs. Plunkett push past the rest of us and go up to him. He was lying by himself on a flat piece of ground holding his face in his hands and squirming side to side. She took his head in her lap and stroked his face while he gazed at her and said some words we couldn't hear. After a few minutes she stopped stroking his head and laid it back down on the ground. Standing up, blood on her hands, looking dazed, she was a sight I'll never forget.

Mr. Plunkett was standing beside us and said, "It don't make no difference to that poor lad who's right or wrong in this war."

I'd never heard that kind of talk before. I figured Mr. Plunkett must be lacking in the patriotic way of seeing things.

Finally one of the soldiers took Mrs. Plunkett by the arm and escorted her back to the wagon train, which was starting to move forward. Nobody said anything for a long time as we walked. I was practically sick to my stomach from seeing all those boys wounded or dead.

We camped that night in the woods alongside the turnpike. Mr. Plunkett said I was welcome to eat with them if I wanted, and I said I was much obliged. Even though the rain had stopped, everything was still damp, so I showed them how they could find dry wood in the trees, and together we built a big fire for dinner. I also contributed my beans and coffee. Mrs. Plunkett made up a whole kettle full of potatoes and beans and another pot for coffee.

Mrs. Plunkett noticed I was wet and cold in my clothes, so she came out with a pile of dry clothes for me to wear. I went into the woods and slipped on a pullover work shirt, canvas trousers, and a raggedy cloth coat. It crossed my mind these clothes would make a good disguise if the sheriff ever stopped me. That idea got me pretty excited, and I thought, *Well, why not go all the way?* So I asked Mrs. Plunkett if she'd give me a haircut like Jimmy had. She didn't want to at first, but Mr. Plunkett told her to go ahead if that's what I wanted. So she did, and when she finished, everybody laughed out loud. There I stood, trousers way above my ankles, sleeves of the shirt and coat too short, and bald as a pear.

But I thought nobody'd recognize me looking like this.

After dinner we sat around the fire and Mr. Plunkett lit up his pipe and took a couple of puffs deep into his lungs and then passed the pipe along to Jimmy and me. I took a few sucks on it but didn't inhale the smoke for fear I'd cough. Back home I smoked a pipe time to time, and sometimes I pulled a mouthful deep into my lungs just to feel the dizziness, but usually I held the smoke in my mouth and snifted it out my nose, which gave a little sting in the nostrils. I noticed Jimmy took it right down into his lungs like his old man. I was mighty impressed.

BANNACK

When Mrs. Plunkett saw I had only one blanket, she said I ought to sleep with Jimmy and one of the younger girls on the same tarp. That was real strange, sleeping with a little girl next to me, but that's what we did, the three of us with a tarp underneath and a big quilt on top and all of us warm and cozy. Didn't take me but a second to fall asleep.

Chapter Four

Next morning I woke with a start and was surprised to see everyone already up and sitting by the fire. Still in the borrowed clothes I'd slept in, I jumped up and joined the family.

"Good mornin to you, Billy," Mrs. Plunkett said and passed me a mug of coffee and a biscuit. My God, what a nice lady she was, and pretty too, with long, light-brown hair tied up in back and a wide smile that'd melt a bar of iron. And she made coffee like nobody else I knew. She spooned the coffee into warmed-up milk from their cow and it was the most delicious coffee I ever drank. I took notice also she put a mite of sugar in mine but not in Jimmy's.

Sitting there drinking that coffee and looking at Mrs. Plunkett, I suddenly realized I had a hard-on pressing like a hot poker against my bare legs. *Damnation*, I told myself, *you've got a beast without a conscience between your legs*. I sat there a long time scared it might show if I got up.

Robins were singing away right above us in the oak trees and the sun was up and shining in a cloudless blue sky. The Plunkett kids danced around me now like they were real happy to have me among them. One of Jimmy's younger sisters who was cute as a button came up to me with a shy smile and said, "Mornin to ya, Billy Mayfair."

My spirits lifted up like one of those hot-air balloons.

BANNACK

We trooped out right after breakfast onto the turnpike heading west, the nine members of the Plunkett family and the idiot that Jimmy said was his father's brother. Mr. Plunkett told the idiot where to walk and to be quiet so's not to bother other people. The idiot nodded and slobbered a little onto his bib.

About noon that day we ambled into a small town that had a scattering of houses and stores on both sides of the turnpike. People were out on the road walking and visiting, and I felt so good I started whistling 'Battle Cry of Freedom." Just as I was at the best part and feeling the most joyous, I saw something that ripped the whistle right out of my mouth. There, up in front of us, was a man stopping the first wagon of our small caravan to ask questions. He was a big fella in a tall hat and wearing a pistol on his hip. A shiver ran through me because there was no doubt in my mind who he was.

He said something to our lead wagon man and looked inside his wagon. Then he walked down to the next wagon and did the same thing. This happened so fast I didn't have time to scamper or hide; I just stood there paralyzed, my heart thumping like a savage tom-tom. Only took him a few minutes before he was talking to Mr. Plunkett.

I could hear him say, "We're looking for a runaway boy stole money from his folks. Warrant out for his arrest." I clenched my teeth real tight, waiting for Mr. Plunkett to turn and point me out. Instead, Mr. Plunkett shrugged his shoulders and said something about not seeing any runaway boy to his recollection.

I was flabbergasted. No older man I knew would stick up for a boy like me against the threat of the law.

The sheriff turned and looked at the rest of us. Even though I wore these borrowed clothes, I was still taller than all the others, and my face was different. I tried to shrink down a bit and avoid his eyes, but I couldn't help noticing that he stared right at me. He bowed his head and rubbed his chin, then looked up at me again and walked over.

"Where ya from, boy?"

Without even thinking I grabbed the cap from my head and said, "Jumpin Jaysus, have ye never seen an Irishman before, sir?" I gave him a little bareheaded bow for good measure.

The sheriff opened his mouth but then just stood there stupefied as if unable to summon words. Mr. Plunkett signaled the wagon train to start, and the whole caravan moved forward. "God bless ye, sheriff," I added as I moved off with the others.

He never said a word but kept looking at me and rubbing his chin. Made me smile to think you can make another man stand aside just by words.

Mr. Plunkett looked at me with a blank face, but I knew he was smiling behind it. I reckoned he must be an outlaw himself at heart. Nobody said a word till we got out of town, then Jimmy started making fun of me. "Jumpin Jaysus, what a terrible accent ye have, Billy. Good thing the man don't know Irish." The kids crowded around me, dancing up and down. "Say somethin more, Billy."

I laughed and patted the five-year-old on the head. Everyone was in a festive mood, and I played along with them, but inside I was still worried. I had glanced back and seen the sheriff following me with his eyes as we disappeared down the road. I figured he was gonna have second thoughts and maybe even send a telegram to the next town saying to keep an eye out for me.

The turnpike smoothed out along this section, and the countryside, woods and fields and grass, reached out flat ahead of us. I reckoned this'd be the last time in a while I'd see this part of the country, and I'd better stare a little closer. Was there something I ought to remember about this land I'd never paid much notice? I stared around pretty good and then reckoned not; I didn't see anything worth keeping in mind.

We saw a farmer now and then riding by in his work wagon, tossing a finger of greeting with one hand while holding the reins with the other. Later in the afternoon one of those fancy-looking stagecoaches clattered by, swaying forward and back on its springs, looking mighty inviting. From the road it seemed like five or six people were inside talking away and enjoying themselves.

BANNACK

I had the money for the coach but knew it would be foolhardy to take one, since the law would be watching all the stage stops. Recollecting the money, I patted myself between the legs just to make sure it was still safe. I had tied it up in a roll with a long piece of string, wrapped the string around my waist and let the roll dangle down in my long underwear next to the beast with no conscience. Speaking of the beast with no conscience, a couple years ago some of the boys and me started making up names for our peckers. My friend Jack Coppedge called his Straight Arrow because it didn't lean to one side, just went straight ahead like old Jack himself. I called mine Boss because it was always nagging me. Pretty stupid, but that's what we were, pretty stupid.

Speaking of stupid things, I'll admit to something even dumber than that. I'm thinking of the time I tried to hump a cow. Me and Jack Coppedge were in the barn at his place one day, slouching around, and I said, "Hell, Jack, I'll bet I can do it." I got up on a bale of hay and dropped my trousers. Then I pulled the cow's tail aside and cried, "Tallyho, Jack!" I stuck it in, and the cow shit all over me. The cowshit went down my bare legs and made a steaming pie right in my open trousers, even left a streak on top of the Boss. Anyway, old Jack Coppedge about died laughing while I wiped off the cowshit.

I don't know why I tell that story because it just makes me look stupid. But what the hell; if I'm stupid, I'm stupid, and I might as well admit it. It don't make me smarter not to tell it.

Then as we were walking down the road something happened that changed everything. Up ahead the lead wagon suddenly stopped, and the whole lot of us had to pull up and wait aside the road. After a while I walked up front and saw one man holding up the leg of an ox showing several others something wrong with the hoof. Sore, I figured. While the men were talking about what to do, a buggy reined to a stop next to them, and a man dressed in a black frock coat and white shirt, like he was going to church, asked if he could do anything to help.

"You don't happen to have a shoe for the brute here," our lead man said.

The man in the buggy shook his head. "Nope. But I'd be glad to give a ride to anyone wants to get up the road to the next town."

I stared at the man in the buggy, wondering if I ought to talk to him. He was a big fella, with a chest like a horse in front and a solid, meaty face. He looked like he could hold off a dozen rebels barehanded. Also looked like an upright citizen.

"How far you goin, Mister?"

He sized me up a minute and replied, "Well, you tell me, son, how far you goin?" When I said St. Louis, he whacked his fist on his knee and said, "That's exactly where I'm goin. And tell the truth I'd love to have some company if you want to ride along." He looked at me real friendly-like.

"Just give me a minute, Mister, I'll be right back." Damn if I wasn't gonna chance it. He looked like an honest fella who wanted some company for his journey.

I grabbed my knapsack from the wagon and told Jimmy and Mr. Plunkett and the rest of the family I had a chance to get to St. Louis faster in the buggy. Mr. Plunkett nodded and said, "We'll miss ye, Billy, you're a good lad."

I was real touched by seeing him and Jimmy and the whole family standing there watching me. Damn if I didn't have to bite down real hard so's not to start leaking tears. I turned and ran back to the buggy, wondering if I'd done the right thing.

Chapter Five

HIS NAME WAS ELMER FUNSTON. Mister Funston to me, since he never invited me to call him Elmer. He was a big talker as well as a big man, and while we bumped along down the turnpike on the cushioned buckboard, he jabbered away as if there was nothing sweeter in the world than the sound of his own voice.

It wasn't a bad voice as voices go. He stretched out his words and spoke in a low-slung tone that rumbled along like the sound of the buggy on the road. He sure had some peculiar ideas, though.

For instance, he said he was an abolitionist, but being an abolitionist didn't stop him from having a colored boy of his own. That didn't make any sense to me, so I said it. "That don't make any sense, Mr. Funston."

He said, "There's a fine point here, son, eludes your grasp. You and I know those slaves down south are treated badly, and so they oughta be free. But it's way different up here in the border states, where we treat those darkies just fine. You take me for instance. I always thought, when I was a boy, that I'd grow up and make myself enough money to buy a nigger. That was my dream. That's an American dream, Billy. So I worked hard, and when I got older, I bought myself a real nice colored boy for eight hundred dollars, and now I don't have to work so hard. There ain't nothin wrong with that, is there?"

I was flabbergasted. I said, "Still seems wrong to me, one man ownin another man."

Mr. Funston held the reins in his right hand. The two horses were trotting along ahead of us at a good pace. From time to time he flicked the reins just to keep the horses mindful he was in charge. He said, "Nowhere in the Bible does it say a man ought not own himself a slave. I'll bet you never knew that either."

He was right there: I didn't know that.

He flicked the reins and didn't say anything for quite a while. We passed through one small village, but it was so quiet no one even noticed us passing through. Then I saw Mr. Funston's face light up. We were riding straight into the sunset at the time and he said, "You see what a beautiful sight that sunset is, Billy, that sun slippin down over the horizon like a big orange in the sky? Well, that's surefire proof to me that God in his glory created the world for us, and after he created the world, he inspired the prophets to write the Bible so's we'd have everything we need to know. And those prophets didn't say a dang thing about slavery. They said we're flawed vessels for sure, and our bodies are tabernacles contaminated by the mud and slime of sin, and that's why we need the everlastin mercy of Jesus Christ to bathe us off. But they didnt say somethin was wrong about havin a slave make your life easier."

He sounded like our preacher back in Ada. I was thankful to my mama for putting me right about him. She pointed out his hogwash before I was old enough to see it for myself. That's one thing I always cherish about my mama: she had a good eye for sizing people up. She could see right through the mush quicker than anybody I ever knew, quicker than Pa for sure.

I think it was because she read so many books. I'm always flabbergasted how many books my mama read. She had a little library in the house, and she'd slip into that world of books and just live there by herself. As I said before, normally she went around looking pretty sad, those large brown eyes resigned to see so much damn foolishness in the world, but when she came out of her world of books, she always had a contented look on her face.

The other thing I ought to mention about Mama was the fact she taught me to read before I went to school. Taught me to read and always asked, like I said before, "What have you learned, Billy Mayfair?" By the time I started school, I was way ahead of all the other kids, so it wasn't long till the teacher had me readin out loud and teachin the others how to read.

While we rode along the turnpike, the remaining daylight turned to dusk, and night began to creep over us like someone up there was turning down the wick. Finally it got too dark to ride any longer, so we stopped in a little village that had an inn along the road for travelers. Mr. Funston asked the innkeeper, a woman about a hundred years old, it seemed, if she had a room for the two of us. She nodded and said, "Only one left. Other two's taken."

After we washed up in our room with an enamel pitcher and basin, we came downstairs for supper. The old lady in her long dress and white apron and funny hat laid out a hot meal for us and four other guests on a big oak table. Boiled potatoes steaming in a big bowl, stewed venison with gravy and onions, dried fruit, cornbread, and coffee.

Mr. Funston offered to say grace, and since nobody objected, he did. I kind of rolled my eyes, expecting to hear the same old stuff again, but this time he added something new. He concluded by saying, "And God bless our sacred Union and boys out there fightin the treasonous rabble from the secessionist states." Now that left a stillness at the table that felt mighty eerie.

Then another fella, also a big man with a full beard and strong-looking face, put his napkin down and cleared his throat. "And I would add, God bless those poor wretched soldiers in the Confederacy out there fighting against Yankee tyranny and dying for what they believe in."

No one said a word. For a long spell you could've heard a pin drop on the tablecloth. Mr. Funston turned to me and said loudly, "Looks like we got a traitor right here in our midst, Billy."

That did it. The other man leaped to his feet and threw back his shoulders. "I'm a man from the North, sir, who believes Mr. Lincoln ought to be searching for peace, not conducting a war against our brothers in the South."

A gasp came from the others at the table.

Good thing the two men didn't have pistols, or there would've been bloodshed. Instead, three other men at the table jumped up and held them away from each other. Mr. Funston kept calling the other man a damn copperhead traitor, and the man shouted back that Mr. Funston was a damn arrogant Yankee who didn't care about the rights of others.

Once they got things settled, everyone sat back down and starting eating supper in silence. It was the best victuals I had in a long time, and I threw it down like a hungry teamster. Mr. Funston didn't say anything, but I could see he was burning inside, and he drank what seemed like half a bottle of whiskey with his food.

Not long after dinner we went to bed. As we were taking off our boots on opposite sides of the bed and climbing in under the blankets, Mr. Funston said, "I got a real treat for you tonight, Billy." He was back in a good mood by this time.

I pulled the blankets up higher over my shirt and trousers and said, "What's that?"

"I'm gonna suck you off, that's what."

I learned something about myself at that moment. I learned my instincts were quicker than my thoughts. I didn't think whether getting sucked off was a favor or not, I just felt sick to my stomach.

"Anybody ever do that to you before?"

The words seemed first to clog up in my throat but finally came out. "No, sir. And I don't want to."

I felt his hand on my leg, patting me like I was a dog. "Well," he said, "I can tell you never did, 'cause if you did, you'd want to do it again." Saying this, he started searching around with his hand for the Boss.

I pushed his hand away and said, "I don't want to do it, Mister Funston, that's all there is to it."

He tried for the longest time, rubbing his damn hand on me, saying just let him have his way this one time, he wasn't expecting anything in return, nothing wrong with getting some pleasure, nobody else was gonna know about it, hell, he'd pay the whole bill that night if I wanted him to.

The more he talked, the angrier I got, till I figured if he went on much longer, I was gonna sock him in the mouth just to shut him up. But I didn't want no fight with him either; I was sure to lose. So I jumped out of bed and said loudly, "You gotta stop talkin like that, Mr. Funston, or I'm gonna find someplace else to sleep."

He got out of bed slowly on his side and stood there glaring at me real steady, a hard-on stretching his long underwear. He took a breath, and his big horse chest expanded. I was scared now and started backing away from the bed toward the dresser, far away from him as I could get.

He came toward me saying, "Why you wanta make this hard for yourself, Billy? You got a easy choice here between hurt or pleasure, whichever you want." His fists were clenched.

I stepped back further and said, "Don't come no closer, Mr. Funston. You're bigger'n I am, and it ain't fair."

While he kept coming, I reached back behind me on the dresser feeling for something to defend myself with. All I could find was the metal pitcher half full of water we'd used for washing. I moved my hand up the pitcher and caught the handle, gripping it hard as I could.

When he reached out his hand to grab me, I swung the pitcher around with all my might and hit him full force against the side of the head. There was a loud metal clang, and he dropped in a heap to the floor without a word. I stood there looking down at him, still holding the pitcher.

Fast as I could, I got into my shoes and coat and stuffed everything else in my knapsack and then stopped dead in my tracks to get my bearings before I left the room. Where was I going, for God's sake? St. Louis, yes, but they'd be looking for me on the turnpike.

When I stared down at him, I didn't know whether he was dead or alive. I leaned down and pinched his nose shut and waited a minute until he finally choked. Thank God he was still alive.

'Course, that meant he'd wake up and beat the piss out of me if I stuck around.

If I stayed on the turnpike west, they'd sure as shooting spot me. The only thing I could think to do was go north a ways and then turn west. I looked around one last time to make sure I got everything, then tiptoed out the door and down the steps to the main floor.

It was pitch dark, so I couldn't hardly see a thing. I wanted to bring some food with me, so I felt my way along the wall to the kitchen and then went in, extra careful not to make any noise. Searching around in the dark with my hands, I found a tin of dried fruit and stuffed my pockets. Then I found half a cooked chicken and stuck that in my knapsack. I let myself out the back door.

When I got to the main road, I cut across and headed directly north through the woods. Lucky for me, the woods weren't too thick, and the moon and stars shed enough light so's I was able to make my way along okay for several miles before stopping to rest. Boy, was I dead tired and cold. I'd left my blanket back at the inn and my good overcoat with the Plunketts.

Still, I told myself, thank God Mr. Funston was alive. Just because he wanted to suck me off was no call to kill him. If I happened to see him again someday, I'd say I was sorry, although on second thought I hoped I was never blessed with that opportunity.

Chapter Six

WELL, THERE AIN'T MUCH TO tell about the rest of that trip to St. Louis, so I'll make it short.

I camped in the woods for three nights on the way westward and ate the chicken and dried fruit and beans and drank my coffee. Mostly beans for three days. People say they don't mind their own farts, it's other peoples that're bad, but I doubt they say that after eating beans for three days.

I made it all the way to the Mississippi River in three instead of four days, and at the river I had to decide which way to go. Easier maybe if I walked down the Illinois side to St. Louis, but also riskier with the law still looking for me. If I could get across the river to Missouri, I'd be out of the reach of the law. So I walked down the dusty road till I got to a village and slipped into the woods to calculate my next move.

It was a small village, I reckoned, of less than a hundred people. A general store with glass windows and a fancy wood façade in front looked to be the only place of business. One of the sayings lettered on the façade was "Ladies Ready to Wear." That struck me as mighty funny, ladies being ready to wear. Besides the general store, there were a dozen or so wood houses along the road and set back in the trees. I watched several people walk in and out of the general store and then sat back under a tree and daydreamed till nightfall. I thought of my mother and sisters and Jack Coppedge and Sara Belnap and wished I'd had a chance to say good-bye to them.

Once it was pitch dark and not a soul stirring on the road, I made my way down to the river and found a canoe tied up alongside a small dock, but naturally there weren't no paddle in the canoe. Fingers crossed, I searched under the dock and sure enough found one stowed away under a tarp in back. Glancing round to make sure no one was looking, I untied the canoe and set out across the river.

Lucky for me, the weather was good, and I could make out lights on the far shore, tiny little specks blinking in the blackness ahead. There was enough light from the moon and stars so I could see the snags in the river and steer around them. No steamers that night, or any other boats for that matter, so I just paddled like hell over the dark moonlit water till I got to the other shore. After tying up the canoe, I caught a few winks in the nearby woods before setting out down the road just after daybreak.

Feeling safer that morning, I walked into the first village I came to and asked about a coach to St. Louis. They said one was coming along later that morning, so I had time for victuals before it arrived. I had a big stack of hotcakes and an hour later took the stagecoach all the way down to where the Mississippi and Missouri Rivers come together at St. Louis. It was dark by the time we got there, but I could see the dancing lights of the city across the water and felt a tingle of excitement. Next day I'd be in the city Pa called the sink of iniquity, teeming with fallen women.

Chapter Seven

ON THE FERRYBOAT CROSSING THE Missouri, I had my first look at how the two big rivers come together there at St. Louis, the Missouri coming out of the west and dumping into the Mississippi going south. It was the most water I ever saw in my life.

The sky was pure blue that morning, the water silvery white, and the sun reached out and put a sparkle on everything it touched. Made me glad I'd left home. Looking across the water at St. Louis, I was struck by the smoke rising in the air from all the chimneys, as if the city was a giant beast giving off steam.

What hit me most, though, as we got closer to St. Louis, was all the boats on the river, hundreds of them it seemed, sailboats, keelboats, flatboats, barges, ferries. What stood out above all were the steamboats, big side-wheelers with their newly painted white decks and high smokestacks puffing black smoke in the air, proud and stately, mighty inviting to a fella on the road for adventure.

Knapsack on my back, I left the ferry and walked along the wharf, where all the ships were docked in a straight row as far as I could see. The levee was six miles long, I learned later. Seemed like a thousand people swarmed across the wide riverfront between the levee and a row of fancy brick buildings three or four stories high facing the river. The row of brick buildings was set back quite a ways from the levee, so there was plenty of space in between for the dockworkers to load and unload crates of merchandise from the boats. I was awed to see so many folks all in one place, teamsters pulling wagons up to the wharf, dockworkers lifting, moving, carrying crates and boxes, and some of them Negroes too. Then there were the dressed-up folks waiting in front of the ships and the passengers getting on and off.

Bells and whistles sounded in the sunshiny air, and a marching band played "The Battle Hymn of the Republic" in front of one of the steamships about to leave. Right in the middle of all this confusion was a fella turning the crank on a box that made music; a monkey tethered by a string danced around in front of him. Damnedest thing I ever saw. I watched awhile, then moved along past a bunch of forty to fifty people just sitting on the wharf looking pretty dirty and bedraggled. I was told they were folks from the war down south who didn't have a place to live.

As I continued through the crowds of people along the riverfront I noticed a young girl standing way up ahead of me in a long raincoat. She faced in my direction and stared at me in a way nearly took my breath away. When I got closer she opened her raincoat and showed me her bare breasts. Maybe she showed me her whole body, but all I saw in that electrified moment were her bare breasts, and they were big as acorn squash.

I just about collapsed on the spot. I swear I was so shocked my knees nearly gave way. But I kept right on walking, my body going forward, but my eyes staying fixed on her breasts till my head was so twisted I couldn't walk and look at the same time. By the time I decided I ought to go back and talk to her, it was too late. She had turned away and was showing her breasts to someone else. This time I noticed the man she showed them to stopped and gave her some money before continuing on his way.

I walked over to a crate and sat down and wondered how much you were supposed to pay to see those big breasts on such a young girl.

By noon I'd made my way up a street called Broadway and moseyed along a boardwalk by a million stores, one after another, many sticking up two and three stories high, some with open doors belching out the smell of smoke and liquor. Most of the buildings were made of wood, but the big ones were red brick. The street was full of wagons and buggies and carriages, and down the center came a single railroad car pulled by two horses on iron rails. Horsecars, they were called. It cost five cents to ride in them. I also saw a milk cart and a coal cart pushed along by boys no older'n me.

The smell of horseshit was in the air, but that didn't bother me. I always thought horseshit smelled just fine till the weather got hot. Then hold your nose, folks.

On one street corner a boy about my age was holding up a newspaper and yelling something about casualty lists from Vicksburg. But what got me, coming from the farm, was all the people waving their arms as they talked, everybody in a hurry, some speaking a language I'd never heard before, men in dark frock coats and tall hats, women in long dresses and bonnets shaped like a shovels in front, Indians in buckskin, and lots of people in ordinary work clothes.

Then all of a sudden the street cleared, and a whole company of Union troops marched by. Right then the bell from the St. Louis cathedral gonged in the distance. Nobody paid much attention to the soldiers or the bell.

Along one side street I saw a bunch a people standing in front of a corral peering over a wood fence at something inside. I thought maybe it was a prize cattle show or something like that, so I walked over to see. What I saw instead, right there in the center of this cattle pen, was a dozen or so Negroes chained together so they couldn't escape. Standing there hatless, their heads bowed under the sun, they looked so raggedy and beaten down, I had to turn away. Never saw anything so sorrowful.

As I walked up the boardwalk, my stomach started to growl from hunger, so I stepped into a cheap-looking restaurant and looked around. At the rear was a stove on which sat a whole panful of sausages giving off a smell that made my mouth water. Right beside the sausages was a big steaming pot of boiled potatoes and a heaping pile of cooked cabbage. The fella behind the counter, wearing a white apron over a big belly, didn't understand my English, so I had to point with my fingers what I wanted, three sausages, a potato, and a big portion of cabbage. Whole thing cost fifty cents.

While I was eating, a fella sat down on the opposite side of the table with a plate of sausages, half a loaf of bread, and a big glass of beer. After a bit we commenced talking, and I told him I was hoping to join a party going northwest to Idaho for gold. The man straightened up and pushed his hat back. He knew somebody, an outfitter down at the riverfront who set up parties of fellas going out.

I found the outfitter sitting on a wood chair on the porch of his store. He looked ninety years old, with pure white hair hanging down to his shoulders and lines in his face like furrows. Must have been a mountain man at one time, I reckoned.

"So ya got yourself a pipe dream, have ya?" he said in a mocking way. "I bet ya got the notion o' comin back rich and makin the girls pull their dresses up. Well, chances are you'll come back all right, but you ain't gonna come back rich, I'll guarantee ya that. Only folks gets rich in the gold camps is the merchants bringin in supplies."

He narrowed his eyes. "Two fellas came in yesterday said they was goin up on the *Emilie* in a couple weeks, and I bet they could use an extra fella. Tell 'em you're not afraid to work and you can shoot straight, and they might take you along. Boone Helm and Jack Gallagher's their names; usually hang out at the whiskey house a few blocks back called Looney's."

That's how I met Boone Helm and Jack Gallagher, although not that day. That day I found a boardinghouse near the riverfront and paid five dollars in advance for board and room for a week, a room I shared with another fella. The landlady was a Mrs. Rhinehart, and she turned out to be sweeter than a mother to me for the rest of my days in St. Louis. She put good victuals on the table, and the boardinghouse had a nice parlor with a fireplace and a small library of books. I saw a copy of *Oliver Twist* which I'd read the year before on another dare from Mama.

The next night I went to Looney's, and the barkeep pointed out Boone and Jack sitting at a table with their legs sprawled out and a bottle of whiskey and two glasses in front of them. I walked up to them and said, "Outfitter down the way says you might take on another hand goin for gold up in Idaho."

They both looked at me from under their wide hats and then at each other. "Hear that, Jack? This nigger wants to go for gold." That was Boone Helm, and he looked big enough to wrestle a bear. He had a thick black beard, long stringy hair sticking out below a dusty old slouch hat, and a greasy buckskin shirt with denim trousers.

"How old are ya, boy?"

"Sixteen tomorrow."

"Jesus Keerist, you hear that, Jack, this chile's goin on sixteen tomorrow." He pushed back his hat and stared at me. "Looks like you aint even shaved yet."

He hit a sore spot there. I had a bit of fuzz on my upper lip and jaw, but I hadn't shaved yet and was embarrassed to admit it.

Boone Helm grabbed his glass, poured a splash of whiskey from the bottle on the table, sucked up a mouthful of tobacco juice and spit it into the whiskey, then handed me the glass. "Try this boy. Make your birthday come quicker."

I figured he was testing me and thought, damned if I was gonna to back down. I took the glass and tossed down a swig like I'd been doing it for years. No sooner I threw it down, though, I threw it back up on the floor alongside where he was sitting. Lucky for me, the meat and potatoes I'd had for dinner didn't come up too.

Boone Helm and Jack Gallagher laughed like this was the funniest thing they'd ever seen. Jack Gallagher slapped the table and said, "Least he ain't scared to try." Jack was leaner than Boone and had pockmarks in the hollows of his cheeks and dark eyes. He wore a wide-brimmed black hat with a shallow crown that had a Mexican look to it.

"Let's see ya try again," Jack said. He handed me his glass half full of whiskey but without the tobacco juice. I pretended to take a good swig but only took in a little bit and handed it back to him.

Boone Helm said, "This boy can't drink, he ain't shaved, I bet he ain't even been laid. You ever had sexual congress with a woman, boy?"

I took a deep breath, determined to stand my ground. "Not yet," I said stiffly.

Jack Gallagher had been tipped back in his chair and he now pitched forward and banged down on the floor. "Boone here says he started sexual intercourse when he was eight years old. I don't believe him because he's a liar and a thief, but that's what he says."

Boone spit a wad of tobacco onto the floor. "Listen here, boy, we need a good nigger to haul dirt for the sluices. Looks to me you're tall enough, even if y'are skinny as a toothpick. You dig and push a wheelbarrow all right?"

"You bet."

"You know how to aim a rifle?"

"Yessir."

"Well, that's all it takes, don't it, Jack? What'd ya say your name was? Billy Mayfair. All right, Billy, now lemme ask ya somethin else. Ya got the sixty-five dollars needed for a steamer ticket north to Fort Benton?"

When I nodded, they looked at each other with eyebrows raised. Jack Gallagher leaned forward. "This is what ya do, Billy. You go down to the levee and get yourself a ticket on the *Emilie* goin north on the Missouri to Fort Benton, and then you go out and get yourself a good repeatin rifle. You do these things first before you lose your money gettin drunk". He looked at me real steady. "Sure you don't mind haulin gravel for the sluices?"

Before I could say anything, Boone Helm added, "Ya come back here tomorrow about this time with the ticket, and we'll take ya along. And for good measure, we'll fix ya up a piece of tail for your birthday."

BANNACK

I left the saloon for my boardinghouse and patted the money roll between my legs. Still there. My hide tingled to think of going northwest with a pair of roughs like that. They looked more like road agents than miners, but that wasn't all bad either considering the wilderness we were headed for. My pa woulda throwed a fit, say they were no-good rotten apples. You live alongside them, you get rotten, too. It made me smile. But I said to myself, *So what, Pa? They're hell-raisers, not church-goers like you.* I always felt like a hell-raiser myself.

Chapter Eight

Standing at the door of Looney's saloon I could hardly believe my eyes. There was Boone Helm and Jack Gallagher, and between them at the same table was a fancy-dressed woman with pale white skin and blond hair down slick to her shoulders. My heart thumped. Was this the lady going to introduce me to sexual intercourse?

The barroom was quiet, only two other tables with customers: one with Union soldiers, coats and hats on the table next to them; another with fellas wearing caps like they worked on the river. Two green baize faro tables were empty, just racks of cards sitting there.

At first I couldn't see the lady's face because she was looking away, but as I got closer and she turned, my spirits sank like a lead sinker. This wasn't the kind of girl a boy had in mind when he jacked off in his hanky. This woman had a puffy face with a lot of powder on it, shiny red lipstick, and eyebrows that looked like they were painted on.

By the time I got there, I was hoping to heaven she wasn't my birthday present.

"Lookee that, Jack, this nigger's got hisself a rifle," Boone Helm said. "Lemme see, Billy."

I was carrying a Henry repeating rifle I'd bought at a gun shop secondhand for thirty dollars earlier that day. I handed Boone the rifle but kept swiping glances at the lady sitting between him and

Jack Gallagher. Looked like she'd been run over by a harrow, she had so many wrinkles tracked through the powder.

Boone Helm stared at the rifle, weighed and turned it in his hands. "Sixteen shots a minute, can't beat that." He took aim down the barrel of the gun, cocked the trigger, and slowly wheeled it around the room as if looking for a target. I figured the rifle was empty, but I wasn't sure. He finally stopped and put a bead on a bottle of whiskey one of the soldiers was lifting to drink. "I'm bettin this here rifle ain't loaded." He pulled the trigger and blew the bottle to pieces in a roar of gunfire. The soldier was left holding the neck of the bottle, whiskey all over his face and uniform.

"Jesus Keerist!" Jack Gallagher cried. "I oughta took that bet."

The fella with whiskey on his face and uniform jumped up and wiped it off with his sleeve. He looked over at Boone and bellowed, "Ya damn fool, ya coulda killed me." The four others were also on their feet, and all five of them started coming at us madder'n hell.

Boone rose up calmly from his chair and held the rifle on them. "You boys better stop right there, y'hear."

All five stopped in their tracks. They were about ten paces away from the four of us. Jack Gallagher and the woman and I were sitting at the table, and we got up slowly. My knees were shaking.

The tallest of the soldiers looked snarling mad and said, "He sounds like a damn secesh to me."

Boone held the rifle steady on them. "I ain't no goddam Yankee, that's for sure."

"Hear that, boys? He's a damn secesh if I ever saw one." The man with whiskey still dripping from his face said, "He ain't got no more bullets in that rifle."

Boone took careful aim at this man. "Anybody come closer, and we'll see if there ain't no bullets left in this here rifle."

Before anybody made a move, the barkeep rushed in between the two groups, shouting for everybody to shut up and get the hell back down in their chairs. He had an ax handle in one hand and was pointing it at the tables. "Get back down, or you'll end up in jail!"

Still holding the rifle on the soldiers, Boone said, "Billy, buy 'em another bottle of whiskey. It's yer goddam gun done it. One for us too while you're at it."

They turned away, and the four of us sat down at our table. Boone had a smile on his face like he was pleased as a pig over the whole thing. "We shoulda taken on all five of them," he said.

The woman shook her head. "You got a brain about the size of a rat's asshole, Boone Helm."

I bought the soldiers another bottle of whiskey, and I brought one back to our table too. But I was starting to get worried about money by this time. Jack turned to me and said, "Well, Billy boy, you get that ticket on the *Emilie*?"

I was all ready for the question. That morning I had located the ticket office on the riverfront and bought a space on deck of the *Emilie*. Just like they said, sixty-five dollars for a space on deck. It would've cost a hundred dollars for a cabin. The ticket agent said the ship was sailing in two weeks.

I pulled the ticket from my pocket and proudly held it up. What I didn't say was how much money I had left. After buying my ticket and rifle and the whiskey, I only had about eighteen dollars left.

"Well, I'll be damned," Jack Gallagher said, slapping the table. "Looks like you're goin with us, boy."

We got to talking about going north to the placers and how much gold was just waiting along the streams for us to dig up. "Some fellas say you pull up a bunch of sagebrush, and the gold falls off the roots," Boone said. He pushed the whiskey bottle over in front of me. "Drink up, boy, put hair on your face." He laughed and reached over and ran his fingers across my jaw as if searching for a trace of hair.

I took a sip of the whiskey and gagged on it. The woman noticed this and got up, walked to the bar, and came back with a glass full of what she said was raspberry vinegar and water. "You drink this down right after you take a swig of whiskey," she told me. I took a sip of whiskey and before I had a chance to gag threw down a gulp of raspberry vinegar and water. The whiskey set off a blast through my whole body, but I held it down. I smiled and after a few minutes took another larger swig and followed it quick with the vinegar and water. I banged the glass on the table and smacked my lips. It felt like a prairie fire was just blowing through me.

I stole a glance at the lady and thought, hell, she wasn't so bad. Underneath all that powder and paint there was a pretty face once upon a time. Still, I was glad she was not my birthday present.

Then Boone said, "Well, Mavis, you ready to demonstrate to this here boy man's greatest pleasure available to rich and poor alike?"

I tensed.

"I don't know why not," she said, winking at me. "He's a handsome boy, I'll say that for him. What you think, Billy, boys here say you ain't done it before. You ready?"

I straightened in my chair and took a deep breath. "You bet."

With this she got up from the table. "C'mon Billy, I'll show you how to ring the bell without even goin to church."

I followed her. Hell, she'd been pretty once upon a time, that was better than never, and more important, she was a woman, for God's sake. I was blessed with a chance to cast my seed where it belonged. As she walked ahead of me, I noticed her body wasn't constructed so bad. Her butt slid side to side, and her blond hair looked smooth as corn silk, her pale white skin nice and soft.

She said, "Wait a second," while she went behind the bar and came out carrying a pitcher of what I soon found out was warm water. We walked upstairs to the second floor and down the hall to a room toward the back of the saloon. It was small, only big enough for a bed and a shelf for a washbowl and oil lamp. When she lit the oil lamp, it cast a blush on her face and a yellow glow on the white sheets of the bed. Just standing there gave me a bristling hard-on.

"All right, Billy, what you got to do business with?"

I started to undo my belt and pull my pants down, but she laughed, "I mean it takes two dollars in advance to do business." I thought, *Wait a second, this was supposed to be my birthday present*, but then the last thing I wanted was to dicker over money. I dug into my pocket and came out with two dollars.

She filled up a tin washbasin with warm water from the pitcher and told me to take my pants down and hold the basin under my pecker while she scrubbed me off first. I dropped my pants and did what she asked, the Boss now burning like a log on fire. Being scared to death of coming too quick, I gritted my teeth till it hurt. She lathered up her hands with soap and then with one hand below and one above began to wash me off. "Looks like you got somethin make a lot of girls happy, Billy." But she hadn't washed more than three strokes when I shot clear across the basin and hit her right in the belly.

"Ay-yi-yi," she cried out and busted into laughter. "You got a quick trigger there, Billy boy."

After wiping herself off and washing me clean, she said, "Well, Billy, you want to try once more the proper way?"

Thank God she said that. All I cared about was getting another chance to do the real thing. I was still hard as a hammer. "Yes, m'am."

She lay down on the bed and pulled her dress up to her neck. I was open-mouthed and wide-eyed to gaze on her long outstretched legs and puffy white belly and mound of black hair parted in the middle. It felt like she had a magnet in there because I was drawn right to it.

Wouldn't you know it, though, the miracle of sexual congress was over in no time. A few times in and out and I spilled forth all that day-dreaming and wishing and wondering in a single blast of jubilation. Years of hankering for one blast of jubilation.

I collapsed onto the bed and looked straight into her soft gray eyes. When I asked where she came from, she said from a farm a ways north of St. Louis. She'd come to town when she was seventeen years old, pure as the virgin snow, looking for a job. The first thing she did was fall in love with a fella treated her real good at first—fine clothes and everything—but then said if she wanted to stay with him, she'd have to do what he told her to. So she did, and that's how she got in the whoring business.

She raised her painted-on eyebrows and said, "What the hell, Billy, I make more money doin this than anythin else."

Staring into those soft gray eyes I forgot all about her not being pretty.

After we got up, she washed herself off and then me. I was calmer now that I didnt have a hard-on, so I said, "Boone told me this was gonna be a birthday present."

"Billy, around these parts a man pays for his own birthday present, you have to learn that. Besides, I gave you pleasure twice, didn't I?"

I had to acknowledge that was true.

Then she said something real nice to me. She said, "I like you, Billy, you're the kind of boy likes to give pleasure to a woman, I can tell. You wanta see me again, I'll make a special price for you."

"Thank you, m'am," I stuttered.

Striding back to rejoin Boone and Jack, I felt pretty good about myself, head swelled up bigger than usual, and why not? I'd just become a full-blooded man. Red blood was swishing through my veins now. I had that feeling you get seeing the flag being raised in a strong wind while the band's playing "The Battle Cry of Freedom."

Chapter Nine

"Hey there, Billy boy," Boone Helm said as I sat down at the table, "ya know the best friend a man has out here? Name is Al K. Hall." He slapped the table and laughed.

I looked at him, puzzled.

"Ya don't get it, do ya? Ya dumb sonofabitch." Boone shook his head. "Say it fast, Al-K-Hall."

"I'll be damned," I said and slapped the table just like he did.

The glass of raspberry vinegar and water was still there on the table, so I took a swig of whiskey and chased it down quick with the vinegar and water. Still made me shiver like I'd been struck by lightning. By this time the saloon was swarming with customers, and the air was full of smoke and noise, folks laughing and shouting and even singing at one table. I noticed Mavis was serving whiskey to the Union soldiers, and a couple of other girls stood at the bar looking around for customers thirsty or horny.

Boone and Jack talked about a lot of things, and mostly I listened, taking an occasional slug of whiskey. After a while I felt funny things happening inside. The fire in my belly gave off a heat that left me feeling a lightness in my head, like I was about to rise and fly. Then everything seemed so damn funny I just sat there and grinned ear to ear.

Boone was sprawled back in his chair singing out words I'd never heard before. Jack Gallagher was hollering to some girl at the bar. When I stood up to go to the outhouse behind the saloon, the whole room tilted right in front of me. Damnedest thing I ever saw. I grabbed the back of the chair to steady myself and looked around the saloon. The room blurred and swayed.

I wobbled through the saloon to the outhouse and back without falling down and collapsed in the chair next to Boone. Boone grabbed my shoulder with one hand. "Ain't this the damnedest birthday ya ever had, Billy? You're doin the two most important things a man can do in life, drink and fornicate." He raised two fingers up to my face. "Only one other thing after that—wander till you find another place to drink and fornicate." He laughed and slapped the table. "Jack here'll tell ya the same thing."

Jack Gallagher wasn't paying no heed; he was trying to get the attention of one of the women at the bar. Boone said, "About time you bought some more whiskey, Billy, I'm busted."

I pulled out a one dollar bill from my pocket and put it on the table. Boone grabbed it and said, "You keep doin this, and we'll get along just fine, boy." He threw down another gulp of whiskey and aimed his finger at me. "Now lemme tell ya somethin else. The preachers got it all wrong when they say drinkin and fornicatin's a sin, and ya gotta work hard and go to church if ya wanta go to heaven." He hawked up a gob and spit on the floor. "You ever heard a man callin down from heaven sayin, I'm sure glad I worked hard and went to church and didn't drink and fornicate? Hell no, you ain't. More likely he'd call down and say, You better do a little more drinkin and fornicatin, folks, time's passin.'" Boone's face broke into a big crooked grin. "Who's gonna say a man goes to church is livin a better life than a man goin to a saloon? Ya know what Shakespeare said. A man spends an hour or so struttin around the stage, and then he ain't heard no more. I'll bet ya never guessed a man like me read Shakespeare, did ya?"

I admitted I never would have guessed. But my words were like big cotton balls in my mouth. While I was floundering around in my head, one of the soldiers walked by our table, grabbed my rifle, and threw it to another soldier, who threw it to the barkeep. All this happened in a couple seconds before Boone and Jack knew what was going on. I reached over and grabbed Boone's arm, but it was too late. The tall soldier slapped Boone across the back of his head and yelled, "Get up, ya damn rebel."

That did it. Boone and Jack got up on unsteady legs and faced four men standing in front of them. The four men were weaving from drink, but they had their fists clenched like they meant business. Then I saw the other one. The other soldier was right in front of me looking like two people instead of one. I didn't want no fight, I wanted to put my arm around his shoulder and be a friend.

He grabbed my shirt and pulled me to my feet. By this time I knew I was in trouble, so I said, "Listen friend, I ain't got nothin 'gainst you." With that he socked me right in the eye, and I went sprawling to the floor. I got up resolved to fight back, but before I had a chance to raise my fists, he whacked me again in the face, and I went crashing to the floor. I don't remember a single thing after that.

I guess it must have been three or four hours later I woke up lying on the dirt floor of the jail. It was dark, and I hurt all over. As I lay there with one cheek on the floor, I felt so sick to my stomach I puked right out the side of my mouth and nearly gagged on my own vomit. It tasted so bitter it burned my mouth and lips. I looked around to see if anybody noticed, but all I saw was a bunch of men sprawled out on the floor or leaning against the bars of the jail in their dirty beards, torn clothes, battered hats, all looking whipped and beaten down. Everybody was dead to the world.

Without thinking I reached down to feel between my legs for the roll of money and found nothing there, not a single bill. Somebody stole my last bit of money. I grabbed for my shirt pocket and felt the outline of my ticket on the *Emilie*. Thank God. Still, I was flat broke. All I could do was grit my teeth and cuss like a teamster.

Boone and Jack were scrunched down against the bars of the jail, snoring so loud they'd wake the dead anywhere but here. Not here, though, because this was the drunk cage, and a half dozen others were snoring away just as loud. It was a whole choir of drunken snores. Only thing interrupted the music was an occasional snort from someone catching his breath, and then he went right on snoring. Just add a pipe organ, and this'd be a chorus from hell.

That was how it felt too, like I'd wakened up in hell. Boone would say, Don't matter, sometimes there's hell to pay for having fun, but I'd had enough of this kind of fun. I resolved then and there, jail was a place I never wanted to visit again. So except for one time to fetch my rifle, I stayed away from Looney's for the rest of my twelve days in St. Louis.

What I didn't know was I'd acquired a taste for whiskey that cut two ways: it would give a lot of pleasure but take away a lot of self-respect.

Chapter Ten

THANK GOD FOR MRS. RHINEHART.

When I came back to the inn that morning, all beaten up and bloody and feeling like a no-good snake in the grass, Mrs. Rhinehart took one horrified glance at me and went right to work. She washed the blood off my face, cleaned out a couple of cuts, and told me to take a bath and change clothes while she fixed breakfast.

She was a big woman with real big breasts, and when she bent down in front of me with her arms raised, I found those big breasts of hers staring me right in the face. They were so huge and the crease between them so long, my eyeballs nearly popped out. I forgot to breathe there for spell. Also, my hands started to sweat, and I must have gone deaf because I didn't hear a thing she said. All I could think was to lean my face up against them, so I did. I leaned forward and let my lips touch her dress. She didn't seem to notice, so I leaned a little more and felt those breasts give like a sponge. Sent a tingle right through me.

She grabbed my ears and looked me right in the eyes. "You're like a frisky little puppy, Billy, sticking your nose in places where it doesn't belong."

While I ate breakfast, she said the most important thing was to find me a job. And it just happened she knew exactly where I could get one, if I was prepared to work hard. I was feeling pretty shaky, but I said I was.

So after breakfast we set off in a horsecar to the Jefferson Barracks north of town, where she worked as a nursing volunteer in the Union hospital. We passed through one section of town that had neat red brick houses lined up along the street with white stone steps all scrubbed and clean. Mrs. Rhinehart said this was the German part of town, spick-and-span compared to the way the Irish laid waste to their part.

As we approached the hospital, she said, "Don't fret, Billy, they need help here so badly, they'll hire anybody who can mop a floor."

The place where Mrs. Rhinehart worked was called a ward. It was a long, thin building with a nursing and supply area at one end, an iron stove at the other, and two rows of patients in between. She introduced me to the head nurse, who wore a white apron over a dark gray dress and a white bonnet. The head nurse looked right away at the bruises and cuts on my face, touched her fingers around my black eye, and asked where I got that, but before I could answer, she said never mind, she didn't have time to talk about it.

The job paid fifteen cents an hour and went ten hours a day, from eight in the morning till six at night, with a rest at noon. Nine dollars for a six-day week. The first thing she wanted was for me to sweep and mop the floor; after that, I was to whitewash the walls. Beyond that she expected me to fetch things for the surgeon and nurses and tend to the operating area twice each day. Tending to the operating area, I found later, meant cleaning up and hauling away arms and legs cut off during surgery.

The nurse ended by saying if I was lazy and came in late, she'd fire me. She meant business.

Within ten minutes I was sweeping the floor of the ward. It hadn't been cleaned in a while, and there was a lot of dirt and dust, not to mention old bandages, scraps of paper, and spills on the floor. There were about eighty soldiers lying in their narrow iron beds with heads to the wall, and I swept around them and down the center lane. It felt real eerie at first, the way those soldiers stared at me with glassy eyes. They were all between fifteen and twenty years old, right around my age.

As I worked around one of the beds, I noticed a soldier staring at me a special long time. He was only a year or two older, and when I looked at him, he said, "What's your name?"

I said, "Billy," and he said his was Luther. His voice was so soft and quiet I could hardly hear him. Seemed like it was hard for him to talk.

He motioned me to come closer, and when I was standing right alongside his bed, he reached over and took my hand in his. His skin was pale and sickly white, and his hand was feverish and wet against mine. Although he seemed weak as a baby, he gripped my hand real hard. I didn't know what to say, I felt so funny. Finally I said, "Where's it hurtin?"

He kept holding my hand, but with his other one he carefully pushed down the sheet till his whole chest was bare. And right there in front of me, clear as day, was a dark red bullet hole on the left side of his chest. Nothing else, no bandage on it, no blood, just a little round spot where the bullet had drilled into him. I compressed my lips and said real softly, "Jesus."

He looked right into my eyes. "The doctor says I'm gonna die."

Hearing that, I went weak in the knees. I gripped the broom harder in one hand while I still held his in my other and said, "Maybe he meant later, not now."

"He meant now," Luther said.

I didn't know what to say, so I just stood there. Seemed like that's all he wanted, to hold my hand and look at me with those eyes that seemed scared as an animal in a trap. Pretty soon the head nurse came up to us and said, "You'll have to get back to work now, Billy." I tried to extract my hand from his, but he held on real tight. She came over and pried my hand loose.

She told me to follow her back to the nursing area at the end of the ward, and when I got there she turned and put both hands on her hips and said sternly, "I don't mind you showin kindness to the patients, Billy, but you got a lot of work to do." Then her face softened, and she added, "God knows they need somebody who loves 'em, but you got to be careful."

I nodded and wondered what she meant. She added, "Just so you'll know, the soldier you were talking to is a German boy got hit by rifle fire in a recent battle west of St. Louis. He's dying, I'm told by the surgeon. Probably won't last through the night."

"Is he hurtin?" I asked.

"The doctor gave him some morphine."

I went back to work shaking my head.

By the time I'd finished sweeping and then mopping the ward, it was lunchtime. I'd talked with probably a dozen soldiers, and they all wanted to tell me where they came from and why they were in the hospital.

One soldier told me half of the patients in the ward had diarrhea. Which meant they couldn't keep anything in, so they got weaker and weaker till some of them just dried up and died. He said diarrhea was killing more soldiers than battle wounds. I noticed he had the same glassy eyes and ashy skin as Luther's. And when I asked him what was wrong with him, he said diarrhea.

'Course a bunch of them had battle wounds. One soldier had a big bandage over the top of his head where he'd been shot, and he was paralyzed all down one side. Another one had a thick bandage covering his arm and was scared of infection setting in. He said he was luckier than the soldier next to him, who'd been shot in the knee, and the infection was so bad he was going to have his leg amputated next day. As he said this louder than need be, the soldier in the next bed glanced over with the eyes of a scared rabbit. I wanted to say something to him, but what?

Anyway, nothing like this had ever happened to me before, so by lunchtime I was feeling a lot more than just hunger in my stomach. Not sick, like the whiskey made me, but an eerie and empty feeling. Since I didn't have any money for lunch, I went back to the kitchen and told one of the cooks. He gave me two raw turnips to eat. So I went out behind the ward and sat with my back to the wall and my face in the sun and munched those delicious turnips.

That afternoon I learned how to whitewash a wall, although nobody taught me, I just did it after the head nurse showed me where all the materials were. I turned the brown wood planks into clean shiny white. By the end of the day, I had done about a quarter of the ward and was plumb exhausted.

Of all the soldiers I'd talked to that day, the one kept coming back to mind was the boy I saw with the bullet hole in his chest, Luther. So just before I left that night I stopped by his bed one more time. His eyes were closed like he was asleep, so I just stood there a few minutes and stared at him. His chest was still bare and the bullet hole was still right there in plain sight.

I was about to go when he opened his eyes and said, "Hello there." Before I could say anything, he added, "I'd like to ask a favor." His voice was soft as a feather, his eyes dark and set back in his head. "Can you find a Lutheran pastor for me?"

His voice was so weak, I wondered if he might slip away right on the spot. I also wondered why he didn't recognize me, since I'd told him my name earlier in the day. "I'll try," I said and dashed back to ask the new head nurse where I could find a Lutheran pastor.

She remembered there was a Lutheran church about ten blocks away, and I might try there. So I ran all ten blocks and arrived at the church about eight o'clock that evening. The church was locked and dark inside, and the little house in back was empty. I found a neighbor next door and asked where I could find the pastor, but she thought he'd gone on a trip to visit several nearby villages and wouldn't be back until the next night at the earliest. I told her why it was important, but she looked helpless and said she didn't know where else I could find a pastor.

So I ran all ten blocks back to the hospital and busted into the ward breathing hard. When I told the nurse I had failed, she said never mind; she had seen Luther a few minutes earlier, and it looked like he wasn't going to wake up again anyway. But I was free to see him if I wanted to.

I stood beside his bed while he slept and noticed how weak and shallow his breathing was, like a whisper. For no reason I said, "I'll see you in the morning, Luther," and he opened his eyes. He looked dazed and confused. He motioned with one finger to come closer so I walked right up next to him in the bed. He took my hand again in his like he did that morning, then closed his eyes and held tightly to my hand for quite a spell. His eyes still closed, he said, "I'm mighty glad you're here, Pastor."

"I'm sorry Luther," I said, "but the pastor…," and I stopped talking.

In his faint voice he whispered, "I wanna ask you somethin. I've done a lotta wrong things in my life, and I'm afraid God's gonna be angry at me." As he said that, his eyes opened wide and seemed to grow even larger as he stared at me. But he wasn't seeing me, he was just staring right through me.

I tried to say something, but the words dried up in my throat.

"Do you think God's vengeful, Pastor?"

His words were feather soft, but they nearly knocked me over. I was flabbergasted. I knew what vengeful meant, but I didn't know whether God was vengeful because I never gave him much heed. I reckoned Pa spent enough time thinking about God for the two of us. But I wasn't so stupid I was gonna tell Luther he was doomed to face a vengeful God either. So I took a deep breath and tried to sound a little like our preacher back home. I said, "No, Luther, God's not vengeful. I know that for a fact." I took a deep breath before going on. "It's God's business to be kind to folks, Luther, that's what he's there for. Especially to fellas like you been fightin on his side in this war. Are you hearin me?"

"Yessir," Luther said in a wisp of sound. "I thought so all along, I just wanted to hear you say it." He closed his eyes again.

I stood there quite awhile feeling sad for Luther. But I was also feeling pretty proud about myself for what I done. Even though I had this big lie on my conscience. Didn't make sense, feeling good while telling a lie.

Luther didn't open his eyes again, so I left and took the horsecar back to the inn. I sat in one of the wooden seats and stared out the open window into the night. We passed by several breweries and factories located on the outskirts of town, but they were dark this time of night. As we got closer into town, the gas lights began to appear alongside the road. Seeing a man set his ladder to one of the poles, climb up, open the window, and light the gas made me wonder where the gas came from. Some folks were out in front of their houses talking and laughing, but I hardly noticed. I was dog tired, and my head was boiling over with thoughts about the day behind me, the soldiers I'd met, and the fear and suffering I'd seen. Especially I thought about Luther and that small red hole in his chest.

As the horsecar got closer to Mrs. Rhinehart's boarding house, there were many lights in the streets and more people outside. As we passed down Green Street, I took notice of several women on the boardwalk all dressed up in tight dresses, trying to coax men to come over. They were standing right in front of a house where several other women were leaning out the window on the second floor, waving at men going by. I guess Pa was right about St. Louis being a town was full of fallen women.

What was really flabbergasting, though, was so much happening to me in such a short spell a time. Seemed like I went long stretches on the farm and nothing happened. Now more things happened in two days than in ten years on the farm.

Chapter Eleven

NEXT DAY I CAME TO work, and Luther's body was lying on top of his bed, wrapped up like a mummy, waiting for someone to cart it away. Seeing it there like that gave me a shiver. The head nurse came over and put her hand on my shoulder, said I'd better not let this bother me too much or I couldn't do my job.

I went out to fetch my stuff for whitewashing, and when I came back, two orderlies were lifting Luther's body onto a stretcher and carrying it off the ward. Just like that! One day I'm holding his hand, and the next he's being toted off like a piece of litter to be thrown away. Damnation, what a thought!

That job in the hospital grabbed my attention all right, and it set the course for the remainder of my days in St. Louis. Eleven days I worked there from eight to six and oftentimes stayed many hours in the evenings talking with the soldiers.

Because my work there got such a hold on me, I never saw Boone and Jack again till we met on the steamboat. I did stop by Looney's saloon and pick up my rifle—lucky for me, it was there—and I did see Mavis again but not for sexual congress.

What I also found out was Mavis had left me with a surprise present. It came on my fifth day working in the hospital while standing at the most unlikely place you can think of, at a urinal trough. The present was a lightning bolt of pain right in the pecker, so powerful it nearly made me scream. It felt like there was a long piece of prickly pear cactus inside the Boss, and every drop of pee pulled the cactus out with it. The pain was such I had to start and stop about four times to get through peeing.

The physical pain wasn't the only part either. That damn disease took away all the good feelins I had about working in the hospital.

At first I was so stupid I didn't connect the pain in my pecker to my sexual congress with Mavis. What crossed my mind right away was God's way of paying me back for the sin of fornication. I could hear my pa shouting, "Divine retribution, Billy!" But that didn't make any sense. How in thunder would God have time to pay back all the men who fornicated? Or if he did, half of mankind would be out of business. So I figured it wasn't likely God did it.

I endured the pain two or three days, till I couldn't stand it any longer, and then slunk over to the surgeon on my ward. He asked if I'd been fucking whores in town, and when I told him about Mavis, he laughed. But it wasn't really a laugh, it was more like a bark. "That'll teach you," he said, his hard gray eyes piercing into me. "Half those whores in this town have the clap."

His name was Wendell Milliken, and everybody said he was tough as a piece a buffalo hide. He told me a case of clap never killed anybody. "Think about it like a bad cold, Billy. It'll get better by itself, like most things do."

Old Milliken worked in the operating area just outside our hospital ward. The operating area was in a tent held up by high poles in the center, staked down by ropes on the sides and open all around. Every time I looked into the tent, it seemed to be half-full of soldiers lying on the ground on stretchers waiting their turn for surgery. Right in the center of the tent was the operating table where Milliken worked for hours on end.

He also liked to brag that only one of four boys he operated on died. "Which is a damn sight better than all four dyin," he said.

One time I stood watching while he finished his work for the day. His face was tired, his shoulders sagging like they had weights on them. His white apron was covered in blood, and so were his hands and arms. Although he held out his hands now and again for one of the assistants to pour water over them, the water still didn't get all the blood off.

After finishing the next to last patient, he didn't even bother to put the knife down on the table. He stuck it in his mouth while helping the orderlies hoist up the last one of the day. He looked like a pirate, with that knife in his teeth and his apron and hands all covered with blood. He even kept the knife in his mouth while he gave the screaming soldier a dose of chloroform to quiet him down. Then he took the knife out of his teeth and started carving off the poor boy's right leg.

After he finished, the orderlies carried the patient away, and Milliken tossed his knife aside, turned around, and rested both hands on the table behind him. He stood that way for a long moment, and then I noticed his shoulders started to shake. He was crying. His body shook like a man possessed while the tears ran down his cheeks.

Chapter Twelve

TRY WHITEWASHING A WARD SOMETIME, then mopping the floor and cleaning up the operating area, and in between times fetching bandages for the nurses and treats for the soldiers. Well, you do that, you don't have much time to feel sorry for yourself. And then seeing all those soldiers suffering and dying, that made a little case of the clap seem like a pittance.

For instance, I got to know one soldier who had a bad case of diarrhea. His name was Harris Williams, and like me, he was from Illinois and grew up on a farm. We had some lively times swapping stories, and each time I saw him he seemed to get a little better. Then, I guess it was on the fourth or fifth day, he told me his mother was visiting and bringing him a big pot of her pork and beans. He licked his chops saying those words. Then he said the doctor wouldn't like that because the doctor wanted him sticking to a diet of godawful tasteless food. But what the hell, he knew his own self as much as the doctor did, and he knew that pork and beans would raise him up like Lazarus.

I wasn't at his bed when he ate all those pork and beans, but I watched afterward when he started vomiting and screaming, and the doctor and nurse rushed over to him. His mother was standing there scared to death, and the doctor told her to leave while they tended her son. I found out later why they told her to leave. Seemed like all that food was such a shock to Harris's body, he couldnt stand it. Well, he went into convulsions and died that afternoon.

I never knew what happened to Harris's mother. The head nurse said she stumbled out in a state of shock, couldn't even walk straight. It sure left me feeling bad for her and Harris.

But the soldier I got to know best was Harold Boykin. One day he called to me while I was mopping around his bed and asked if there was a chance I could read him something. His face had that same ashy white color and looked to be shrinking and shriveling because of his illness. It was a terrible thing to see, the faces of those boys shrinking down to where you could see the outline of their skulls. Anyway, two weeks earlier, Harold had been shot in the foot in a battle down south, and because nobody took care of the wound in the field hospital, he'd come to our hospital with a bad infection and a high fever.

I said, "No, I don't have time to read because I've got too many things to do." I went on working that afternoon, but it bothered me so much, saying no, I went back to see him after work and said I had a copy of *Oliver Twist* back at the inn if he wanted me to read that. He busted out in a big smile.

To make it short, that next night I started reading *Oliver Twist*. I sat in a chair at the foot of his narrow bed, and he sat propped up with his legs crossed on top. A few other soldiers heard me reading and came over to listen, and before long there must have been a dozen soldiers sitting around Harold's bed listening to me read. Just like it was in school when the teacher had me reading to the younger kids. Those kids loved to hear me read, and so did the soldiers. They never said a word till I finished each night, and then they couldn't stop thanking me.

Reading the book was only the beginning of my friendship with Harold. I discovered he was from Ohio and had gone to college two years at a school called Oberlin. He had a deep fondness for that place, saying it was the only college he knew of where boys and girls studied side by side.

Next few days, we had several long talks, and I was flabbergasted to learn how many books he'd read. Besides books like *Oliver Twist* and *David Copperfield* which I knew about, he had studied philosophers whose names I'd never heard before—names that sounded like Daycart and Shopenhower. I told him I'd finished secondary school and had heard the word philosophy but didn't know exactly what it meant.

He said, "Just think about a little pocket compass, Billy. You know how a compass points north all the time. Well, you know it points north, but you don't know *why*. And the reason you don't know why is because what makes it do that is invisible. Philosophy is about understanding those invisible things that make visible things do what they do. And that includes understandin why we do what we do. You get what I'm sayin?"

I didn't, but I was all ears.

"That's why it's so interesting," he said, nearly breathless from his own excitement. "My professor at Oberlin says philosophy is a love of learning, and he says learning is a great adventure, just as much as you going to the gold fields."

These words set my head spinning, but it wasn't just the words. It wasn't even mainly the words. Mainly I was struck by Harold himself, the way he got himself all excited just telling me what he knew. You'd think he'd just been offered a chance at sexual intercourse with the queen of France.

Anyway, after that I visited him every chance I got till the day I left.

One afternoon our hospital was visited by a bunch of society people from St. Louis. They drove up in their fancy barouches and stepped out into the spring sunshine in their fine clothes, ladies in their long swishing dresses and men in frock coats and top hats. They talked and laughed among themselves and stepped lively into the hospital like they were going to a ball or something.

The head nurse escorted them down the center of the ward, and they smiled and said hello to the soldiers lying there staring in stupefaction. One of the soldiers told me later he felt like a monkey in the zoo. When they finished their tour, one gentlemen in especially fine clothes stepped forward at the end of the ward and made a little speech.

"I'm proud," he said, "to see soldiers with such courage and fortitude. I can promise you, we pray to God every day for you and your comrades who have fallen in the noble cause of preserving the Union." After he finished, the soldiers lay there stony-faced and glassy-eyed. The silence in the air made me a little discomfited. Harold looked paler than usual. He glanced up at me and said under his breath, "I used to think I wouldn't mind dyin for a noble cause, Billy."

Even though the soldiers didn't think much of the society people, I could see the society people thought highly of the soldiers, and what they did was leave a sizable contribution of money for treats, which the soldiers enjoyed a lot. I recall one soldier asking if we had any horehound candy; he was dying for a taste of horehound candy, so I got him some from the treats bought by the society people. Another boy asked me for licorice, several others asked for tobacco, others for a drink a cider or lemonade. Thanks to those society people, I was able to get these things for the soldiers.

All through my last days there I got to know Harold Boykin better. Some nights, after reading, I'd stay and continue a conversation with him. One night I sat beside his bed while we talked in whispers till nearly midnight. He was all excited about what he was gonna do after he got out of the army. He was gonna work hard and save enough money to travel to Europe and see how other people lived. "Live and work there for a few years," he said. Staring at me with stars in his eyes, he said, "See the world, Billy, that's what I'm gonna do."

I felt uplifted by our conversation.

But I was also bothered by his sickness, and one day I asked the head nurse about him. She said the infection in his leg was worse than when he first came in, and the doctors couldn't stop it. They told her he was gonna die. I felt the strength drain out of me on hearing that and asked how in God's name could anybody die of a wound in the foot. The nurse just shook her head and looked helpless. She said half the soldiers died of diseases and infections they got after suffering battle wounds not bad enough to kill them. "The hospital is a dangerous place, Billy, aside from being a healing place."

That whole conversation left me feeling limp.

By this time I'd gotten to know the head nurse pretty well and liked her. When I told her Harold was planning on going to Europe after the army, she just shrugged and said it was normal, dying patients talking about a future they didn't have. Clara was her name, and she was like Milliken and so many of the other medical workers there. She just didn't have time to be nice. But she was good to me and said I always had a job there if I wanted one. When I said good-bye to her my last night there, she even gave me a hug.

That last night I said good-bye to all the soldiers in the ward and shook hands with every one of them. But I saved my last good-bye for Harold Boykin because we'd become such good friends.

It was late by the time I got to his bed, but he was still awake, waiting for me. I said I had to be leaving for the gold fields the next day and wanted to tell him how much I liked knowing him. He said he wished he could go with me and took my hand in his. Standing there holding his hand, looking into his ashen face and dark eyes, and hearing his weak voice, I knew he was gonna die, and the thought sent a cold shiver through me.

We talked awhile, and then I said I had to go. He pulled down on my hand as if he wanted to whisper something in my ear, but instead of whispering something, he kissed me smack on the lips, and for a long time too. My instinct was to rear back in disgust, but I couldn't. I didn't want to hurt his feelings, and besides, he had a tight grip on the back of my head. But, boy, what a shock that was, a regular lightning bolt right between the ears. I stood back afterward shaking like a leaf.

Staring down into his sad eyes, I saw he was crying, tears spilling out without his face moving or him saying a word. I squeezed his hand and walked away, biting down real hard to stop my eyes crying too. But it wasn't no use, and the tears came anyway.

BANNACK

It was a strange ride home in the horsecar that night. I was in a whole different state of mind from normal, as if I was barely touching the world outside myself. The streets and lights and houses and people passed by in a blur.

I thought of Sara Belnap and recollected how delirious I'd been when we kissed outside the barn one night between dances. I held her tight against me and pressed my lips on hers and burned to have sexual intercourse with her.

Kissing Sara Belnap was way different from being kissed by Harold Boykin. Harold didn't give me a burning desire for sexual intercourse. There was even something disgusting about that kiss, something that made me want to pull back, but it also left me with a mysterious glow inside like I'd been touched by the Lord Almighty. Never felt anything like it before. It didn't make a damn bit a sense. A normal fella wasn't supposed to feel like that from being kissed by another man.

Anyway, as I rode back to the inn that night in the horsecar, untouched by everything outside me, I finally said to myself, *Don't fret about what's supposed to be, Billy, just take what is and be glad about it.*

Chapter Thirteen

As I said, that job at the hospital sucked up nearly all the rest of my days and nights in St. Louis. Only exception to this worth telling was the Sunday afternoon Mrs. Rhinehart took me to a lecture at the German Metaphysical Society. That's right, the German Metaphysical Society. Here's how that happened.

I'd been coming back to the boardinghouse every night after work, and good old Mrs. Rhinehart was always there to put a special dinner on the table for me—the other guests had already eaten by the time I got home—and ask how my day went. Sometimes she laid out a stew, other times sausage and cabbage, but my favorite was a big plate of steaming hot cornmeal covered with syrup and butter and a glass of cold milk from the icebox. I shoveled it down like an untamed savage while telling her about my work in the hospital. She sat there still as a cat and listened to everything I said.

Then one night she stood up and said, "All right, Billy, I see you got a good heart, what you need now is a smart head to go along with it." Then she asked in a sweet voice if I would be so good as to escort her to a lecture by a famous German professor who was going to discuss the philosophy of Benedictus Spinoza.

"Jumpin Jaysus," I said, imitating Jimmy Plunkett, "what kinda name is that? Benedictus Spinoza."

So Mrs. Rhinehart and I went to the lecture on a Sunday afternoon in May. The temperature was warm enough, thank God, so's I could leave that old tattered coat I got from the Plunketts at home. I washed my face and combed my hair and put on a red flannel shirt and black wool trousers and tucked my trousers into my boots, thinking that might add a touch of class. Mrs. Rhinehart said take them out and stop being a hick.

We took the old reliable horsecar to a stop not far from the university and from there walked over to a large building called Wyman's Hall. As we walked, Mrs. Rhinehart told me the Metaphysical Society here in St. Louis was the most famous philosophy society in the country because it was founded by the Germans. The Germans were revolutionaries and freethinkers who came over from Europe to escape the tyrants there. They were good at making philosophy, she said, but they were no match for the Americans when it came to making money.

I asked Mrs. Rhinehart what freethinkers were, and she said, with a sound of disapproval in her voice, they were men who believed in sexual relations outside of marriage, just for love alone.

Well, that sure gave me an itch to know more about freethinkers.

She paid twenty-five cents for her ticket and fifteen for mine, and we stepped into Wyman's Hall, a space bigger than Looney's saloon with a high ceiling and fancy hanging lights and wooden benches lined up in rows. The benches were filled with bald-headed men with gray beards and older women with their hair piled up on their heads and wearing bright new dresses. Not a single person in the audience was my age, and it made me feel I was in the wrong place. Mrs. Rhinehart patted me on the leg as we sat down, as if she knew what I was thinking.

She had on a long-sleeved blue satin dress that went right up to her neck, and since the dress was tight, her huge breasts rode out in front of her like a ship in full sail. Just think of one of those four-masted cutters flying from New York to San Francisco in a record forty-nine days.

Looking around at all the other women made me think she was a good-looking lady, and it was a pleasure sitting next to her. When a man sat down on the other side of me and forced me harder up against Mrs. Rhinehart, the warmth of her body seeped right through my shirt and skin and set a fire in my heart. I suddenly had a wild thought: What if Mrs. Rhinehart became a freethinker and invited me to bed with her? What a thought that was! She'd press those huge breasts of hers against my naked body, and I'd turn into a pillar of fire. I'd set the whole bed ablaze. It took my breath away just to think about it.

A man appeared on the stage about fifteen rows in front of us, and raised both hands for quiet. Then he introduced the speaker, Professor Johann Schilling from the University of Königsberg.

Professor Schilling was a tall, thin man with a clean-shaven face and a thatch of long hair parted in the middle of his head and falling down nearly to his shoulders on both sides. His black coat was buttoned all the way up to his neck. He arranged a handful of notes on the podium in front of him, looked around very seriously at everyone and said:

"Benedictus Speenoza vas born een 1632 unt died een 1677."

That sentence I understood. But from then on I got lost in a jungle of words I'd never heard before. It made me feel dumb as a doornail.

Before long my mind strayed elsewhere. I thought about the steamer *Emilie* I'd be taking in a couple days and wondered what it'd be like meeting Boone and Jack again. I calculated 16 dollars was what I had from my work at the hospital, and when I finished paying Mrs. Rhinehart for everything I owed, I'd have nearly ten dollars to take on the trip. The ticket agent had said I could get a job as a waiter on the ship that'd pay for my meals. Main thing was I had enough money to get all the way to the gold fields.

As I was sitting there daydreaming, I suddenly caught the word *God* in something the professor said. I woke from daydreaming and heard him say the idea of God most people had was all wrong. Christians and Jews alike were mistaken.

Well, that was something I hadn't heard before.

I'm not very smart, and I can't say his exact words, but I can tell you what I thought he said, and what I thought he said was this: God wasn't some fella up in the sky looking down on us and shaking his head in exasperation every time we did something bad. No, God wasn't a fella at all. He was nature, and when we looked up at the sky at night, we were looking right into the face of God.

Well, if that wasn't the damnedest thing I'd ever heard, the sky being the face of God. So I listened as tight as I could, and what I heard him say went something like this:

There wasn't no need to ask God for help, because he didn't give any, no need to be afraid of him because he didn't hurt people, and no need to listen for his marching orders because he didn't give marching orders. Instead, the professor said, God was nature, pure and simple, and since we were part of nature, he was us. So the best way to thank God for being alive was to be nice to each other.

I'd never heard anything like that before, either. It made my head spin just like Harold had made my head spin.

Then the professor went back to saying something I couldn't follow so my mind strayed again. I thought about what he'd said about God, and thought Pa would have a conniption fit.

I noticed Mrs. Rhinehart was listening to the professor so tightly she hardly breathed. Looking at her it crossed my mind I oughta write a letter to Mama. Mama was gonna worry about me, no doubt about that. I wondered what Pa had told her. Probably made me out to be a scoundrel. That's what he was always saying I'd become. But I reckoned she wouldn't believe him.

I couldn't get ahold of anything more Professor Schilling said until right near the end when I heard the words *road to liberty*. That sat me up straight again. It sounded like he said we human beings—"human beinks"—got caught up in a tangle of things that made life worse for ourselves than need be, but there was always a road to liberty that could set us free from all the bother around us. I'd never heard that expression before, *road to liberty*, and even though I had no idea what he meant by setting us free from all the bother, I liked the idea of it being there for us to travel on.

On our way back to the inn in the horsecar, I told Mrs. Rhinehart I was confused about what the professor meant when he talked about the road to liberty. She thought a minute and said, "You're already on it, Billy; just coming here puts you on it. It's not a turnpike he's talking about. Knowledge is the road to liberty."

That night I wrote Mama a letter in my head telling her I was fine and had attended a lecture on the philosophy of Benedictus Spinoza. But I didn't end up sending it.

Chapter Fourteen

IT WAS A SUNSHINY DAY, and the flags were whipping and snapping in the breezy blue sky. A band was blaring away on the wharf, and the ship's whistle tooted every so often as if the ship were alive and wanted to join in on all the fun and excitement. I swear it was a sight to behold to see the *Emilie* sitting there in the water, looking proud as a princess and gulping in passengers as they streamed onboard from the gangplank.

All the noise and bustle and expectation put me in high spirits.

Mrs. Rhinehart had come down to the wharf to see me off and couldn't stop asking if I had everything I needed. 'Course I had everything I needed because she'd seen to it herself, stuffing my knapsack with meat loaf and sausages and black bread and dressing me up in a new blue-checked cotton shirt, saying I needed a cotton shirt instead of those sweaty woolen ones I wore. She fussed, and I squirmed, and finally we hugged each other good-bye. It was the warmest hug I ever got or expect to get the rest of my life. Felt like I was swallowed whole.

Once I was on the deck, I waved good-bye. She shouted from the dock, "You be sure and visit when you get back, Billy Mayfair."

I nodded. I also had a little choke in my throat and had to bite down hard to keep those feelings from turning me into a sissy.

The boat was a side-wheel packet with a wood hull, I learned, and it was busting at the seams from 138 passengers on board. It also had 350 tons of freight and a whole stable full of mules and horses and wagons stowed down below. Fifty-three of us slept right out in the open on the main deck, and eighty-five passengers lived in luxury on the second deck in cabins. The pilothouse sat on the third deck along with two tall smokestacks puffing black smoke.

I noticed a young girl about my age standing at the rail of the second deck with a woman who looked like her mother. They were peering out over the riverfront and waving to somebody. I couldn't see whether the young girl was pretty or not, but she stood out like a lighthouse at night amongst all these other folks.

Boone Helm and Jack Gallagher were sprawled out on the deck with their backs against the rail. As I threw my knapsack and blanket down in the space marked off for me in the stern not far from theirs, Jack shouted at me.

"Hey there, Billy boy. You been stayin outa jail?"

I sat down beside them, and we talked for a long while about what we'd been doing. They'd been hunting south of St. Louis and made money for the trip by selling turkeys and deer and pheasants they'd shot. They also had a deal with the ship's captain to shoot game for the ship's kitchen on our way to Fort Benton.

The second night out Jack told the story of where he'd first met Boone. He was in Idaho Territory at Fort Hall, drinking and scrounging, and at the time didn't know Boone Helm from Adam. In fact, he knew Adam better because of Sunday school. Anyway, while he was in Fort Hall, he heard about two fellas who'd gone out in the wilderness hunting and got caught in an early blizzard. Worst blizzard in years. Nobody heard from them, and after a while everybody thought they'd perished in the wilderness.

Then one day—bright sunshine bouncing on the white snow—Boone came walking outta the woods carrying the leg of his partner over his shoulder. Folks were stupefied. He'd ate his own friend. Couldn't help it, Boone said. They got trapped in a cabin without a scrap of food, and his partner had told him to feed on his remains if God took him first. And God took him first.

He turned to Boone, "You never said if you liked the taste o' human flesh."

"Tasted worse things," Boone said. When he smiled, his teeth looked like a row of blackened corn barely visible through the narrow slit of beard.

Anyway, that's the way it went, telling stories evening after evening. Boone and Jack didn't much like to talk about their personal lives, but I kept asking them questions—Jack said he never knew anyone asked so many questions—and by the time we passed Fort Leavenworth and were steaming north, I got to know a lot about them.

Jack came from a respected old family in Virginia, grew up on a small plantation with a dozen or so slaves who did the field work. But he never liked his life there, never could stand all the straitlaced properness in his family, his sweet-talking mama and his ass-licking papa. Jack was a black sheep from the day he was born, and when he was seventeen, he got one of the girls in town pregnant, and his papa said he had no other choice except to marry her. But he reckoned he did have another choice: he lit out. Damned if he was gonna get himself tangled in marriage. He didn't even like girls except to fornicate with.

Jack said he'd been wandering around the West ten years trying to stay out of trouble and being a miserable failure at it.

Boone told a way different story. He was from Tennessee and grew up dirt poor, his old man a drunk and his ma cranky as a wet hen. Reason he left home was, he got into a knife fight with another fella at a Saturday night dance. Both were full of white lightning and crazy mad. The other fella lunged at Boone and sliced a cut across his arm, but in making the lunge, the drunken fool stumbled forward, and Boone drove a Bowie knife to the hilt into his back. Didn't look good, this fella lying on the ground with Boone's knife sticking out of his back and no witnesses around. He reckoned his choice was either jail or skedaddle. So he skedaddled. There was probably still a warrant out for his arrest in Tennessee, but he didn't give a hoot because he reckoned he was never going back anyway.

Those stories were interesting, but I got discomfited when they talked about politics and the Union. Boone maintained that slavery was founded on the truth known to all civilized men that the Negro was not equal to the white man. He called the President *Abraham Africanus* and said his Emancipation Proclamation was better called a *Miscegenation Proclamation*.

I said he was wrong and quoted Thomas Jefferson as saying all men are created equal. "Besides that," I added, "Thomas Jefferson was the smartest man ever lived."

Boone scrounged through his knapsack and came out with a photo and handed it to me. The picture was all bent, wrinkled, and faded, but it showed two people standing naked, a white woman and a black man, and she was holding his pecker like she was shaking hands with him.

"Look at that," Boone said, "and tell me all men are created equal." I was stupefied. Boone took the picture back and said, "The Negro has an oversize pecker and an undersize brain, Billy."

Jack said, "That's better'n you. You got a undersize pecker and a undersize brain both."

The awful truth was, they were both secessionists, and I had to stand up against them all the way to Fort Benton. Which I did, too. Eventually Jack shrugged and said he couldn't talk to a stubborn idiot like me, ignorant as a damn rock. But I stood my ground, and they respected me for it. I came to realize they didn't really care about politics or anything else except their God-given right to do what they damn pleased. No country, no government, no law, nobody was gonna tell them what to do.

One night I asked them whether they believed in God. Boone said, "Hell yes, I do. I saw him once in New Orleans. He was a faro dealer had a pretty face and a handsome brown beard."

Jack snorted, "I bet he didn't have that gold ring hanging in the air over his head."

"No," Boone conceded, "he didn't have any ring."

Jack turned to me, "Whether ya believe in God or not, Billy, it don't change a damn thing."

BANNACK

The nights were fun, but the days were long. Thirty-one days, from the first part of May to the first part of June, it took to go from St. Louis to Fort Benton. Two thousand five hundred miles up the Missouri River, the captain told us, bucking current all the way.

That meant a lot of sitting and staring.

Oh yeah, I forgot to say, Mrs. Rhinehart stuck a small dictionary in my knapsack which I didn't discover till I was on the boat. Wouldn't you know she'd do something like that, stick in a dictionary. She wouldn't quit trying to improve me. I confess to looking up a few fancy words on the trip just for the hell of it, but most of the time I stayed fixed on what was happening around me.

What was happening around me was mostly nothing. I sat on a crate at the bow of the boat staring at the dirt brown water of the river. Since it was spring, the river was swollen from the runoffs of other rivers and tributaries all the way north to the Milk, each one heaving its brown gush into the Missouri. The Missouri just gulped it all down without a twitch and continued rolling along south and east to the Mississippi. The river carried driftwood, logs, branches, even animals. One day I saw a dead cow float by.

'Course navigation was treacherous, and one reason was the snags. These little buggers stuck their heads up here and there on the surface of the river, streaks of water behind them the only way to tell where they were, looking as innocent as pie in the quiet flow of a peaceful day. But underneath the surface they were tough enough to tear off a paddle wheel. Then there was the surface ripple of water here and there warning of an invisible sandbar or shallow ledge of land sticking out in the river on which a ship could go aground.

So the captain tied up at night, to make damn sure he didn't strike something dangerous in the dark. That slowed the ship down, but it also provided a lot of time for stretching out and letting go. With the boat tied up to trees along the bank, underneath a glowing moon and a sky glittering with stars, folks drank and sang and told stories and danced the night away.

The worst thing about the trip was the pot-licking mosquitoes. They were so thundering bothersome, I had to sleep some nights with my head covered up. Boone said they didn't bother him because they didn't like the taste of whiskey in his blood.

Some days it wouldn't stop raining, so everyone on deck would crowd into the sitting room, moaning about the weather, teeth chattering from the cold. Most days, though, the sun came out, and the air was fresh and clear, and in the blazing sunlight even the river looked clean.

Sitting for hours at the bow of the ship, I noticed the banks of the river were mostly lined with cottonwoods and willows, their leaves shiny green and new in the bright sunshine. When a breeze came up, the river wrinkled in the wind, and the newborn leaves danced and waved from the banks.

Certain places the river narrowed between steep banks and high bluffs on both sides, and the water got deeper and faster, rushing by like it couldn't go fast enough to reach the Mississippi and eventually the Gulf of Mexico. On those days the engines rumbled and the deck trembled from the power of the machines fighting the force of the river.

Other places the river widened and flattened out and slowed down as if it wanted to take a long breath. In these places the banks gave way to longer views of the treeless hills and grassy flatlands of the plains. After the green woods and yellow cornfields of southern Illinois, the country looked barren and empty.

In some stretches the river twisted and turned and slid its way through the land like a moving snake.

After we passed Council Bluffs, the best way to reckon where we were was not by villages or forts but by the rivers we passed. Three of them, the Running Water River, the White River, and the Cheyenne River, took us over halfway; then the Grand, the Little Missouri, the Yellowstone, and the Milk took us most the rest. Jack said these rivers were the turnpikes of the West.

Jack surprised me being so knowledgeable about geography. One day, when we were standing by the rail of the ship and he was sober and serious, he turned to me and said, "Stretch your mind, Billy, and think about this whole big chunk o' land we're passing through.

A great big plain, all the way from the Missouri River to the Rocky Mountains. Then tilt that plain in your mind so it's higher in the west than in the east. That's what it does, it slopes down to the east, so when we get out there to the gold fields of eastern Idaho, Billy, we're going to be higher up than we are here. That's why folks out there look down on people in the East. They got reason to."

He smiled at his own joke.

One day a whole herd of buffalo crossed the river ahead of us, and the captain had to stop the boat and wait till they got by. Must have been a couple hundred at least. Men on board got out their rifles and shot a bunch of them, easy targets splashing helpless in the water, and the crew picked up two dead ones for the ship's kitchen.

One time the ship stopped for a full day at the mouth of the Cheyenne River, and I set off by myself for a hike out onto the plains. It felt good to stretch my legs, and I walked till the river was out of sight and I'd reached a slight rise where the countryside seemed the same on all sides. The blue sky above came down to the horizon even on all sides like a big glass bowl. My eyes reached out in all directions, and I took in more space than I ever had before. Miles and miles of nothing except grass, not a living thing in sight. It looked mighty lonely to me.

Chapter Fifteen

YOU REMEMBER THAT GIRL I saw the first day on board, standing on the second deck alongside a woman looked like her mother. Well, that was Harriet. Next time I spotted her was in the dining salon where she sat with the same older woman at one of the large tables for eight people. This wasn't one of the tables I'd been assigned as a waiter, so I had to mosey over toward hers to swipe a closer look.

Well, might as well say it straight. Harriet wasn't what you'd call pretty. Her two front teeth were so far apart you could stick a toothpick in between without touching either side. She had freckles across her nose and cheeks and frizzy red hair. But there was something so lively in her face that I was drawn to her anyway.

I talked the waiter serving her table into switching with me for one night. Then I stood behind her table while each person marked a menu saying whether they wanted venison or chicken, and when I picked up Harriet's menu, I caught her eyes in mine and stared harder and longer than usual. She didn't turn away; she stared right back, and stared in a way that told me she was no bashful giggling little girl: she had blazing blue eyes could light up a whole room. Later, when I was forking a venison steak onto her plate from the platter I carried, I winked at her. She didn't show a trace of feeling at first, but then later, when I was spooning canned peaches in her dessert bowl, she winked back at me. I couldn't help but break a smile. I'd never had a girl wink at me before.

I kept an eye peeled for her on deck but never caught a glimpse of her that first week. Then one day when I was least expecting it, she found me. I was standing as usual at the bow of the boat, hands on the railing, staring out at the dirt-colored river, and she came up right next to me and stopped, put her hands on the railing, and stared out in silence. Out of the corner of my eye I saw she was wearing a plain blue shirt and blue denim pants—not a dress like you'd expect on a girl—and her reddish hair was parted in the middle on top, fell down straight on both sides, and made a little curl at the bottom. Not long hair, but bouncy. She puckered her lips as if she was pondering what to do next.

I turned to her and said, "I never knew a woman with red hair before."

She laid those gleaming blue eyes on me and replied, "I can fix that for you right now if you want."

We both laughed.

And that's the way it went with Harriet. She was not just funny, she was fun to talk to. I never met anyone I could talk to so much and never run out of things to say.

First thing I learned, she was from St. Louis, and her last name was Chestnut. Harriet Chestnut. I joked about that. "Chestnuts are poison to eat, I hear."

"No, they're mighty hard to crack, that's all." Things like that.

She was about four inches shorter and three years older'n me, at nineteen, and had already spent a year in college. She wasn't too thrilled about her college, though, because it was a girl's school, and they didn't teach science and history, things she wanted to learn more about. They did teach literature, but the books they taught were chosen for their properness, not their interest. For instance, they didn't teach *The Scarlet Letter*, which was her favorite book.

To show you how dumb I was, I thought *The Scarlet Letter* meant something you got in the mail.

She said she was headed for Fort Benton to live with her aunt and uncle for a year. The woman with her was not her mother but her aunt. Her uncle was head of the Featherstone Trading Company located there in Fort Benton and she was going to work for him as a secretary and bookkeeper. She thought it'd be an adventure.

Damn if she didn't have an itch for adventure just like me.

The most flabbergasting thing, though, was Harriet got better looking the more I got to know her. That didn't make sense when I stopped to think about it. Seemed to me it ought to be just be the opposite, she'd get worse looking. But the more we talked, the more I took notice of her quick blue eyes and fine delicate lips. Her lips reminded me of a famous actress whose picture I once saw.

We took to meeting on the deck during the daytime and taking short walks around the boat together, even exploring the stables belowdecks where the horses and mules were kept. And sometimes we even met later at night and danced together at the social gatherings. But these meetings were never in the company of her aunt. She always slipped away to see me after the old lady went to bed.

I'd say the thing I liked best about talking to Harriet was, she was smart, and she didn't try to prettify things. For instance, although she was a Unionist, she hated the war. "If this war was really about slavery," she said, "I'd be for it too, but it isn't. Mr. Lincoln declared the slaves free in the secessionist states, where his words don't have any effect, but he didn't declare them free in the border states where his words would have some effect. There's still slavery in Missouri, Billy, or didn't you notice? This war is about the Union, and that isn't worth all the suffering and dying."

I said, "I think it's about slavery, Harriet."

When we talked about these matters, I discovered I believed a lot of the same things my pa did. Made me recognize he wasn't wrong about everything.

Anyway, Harriet was the first person I told about Mr. Funston trying to suck me off, and I told it without a blush. She thought it was funny and terrible at the same time. Anyway, that's the way she was, I could tell her anything.

So I told her about Boone and Jack and how they were no-good low-life Southern renegades. She said she'd rather meet a straight-talking lowlife than a high-life hypocrite.

On the day I introduced her to Boone and Jack, they were cleaning their rifles for hunting antelope and deer the next day. Boone looked up from his place on deck and said to her, "Ya got that red hair on your pussy, too?"

"Yep," she said, staring at him.

Boone said, "I hear redheads buck harder'n others."

"I don't know about that, Mr. Helm, but I know they're mighty quick to recognize a dirty-talking man who says things just to shock a girl."

Jack Gallagher and I clapped.

Boone looked at Harriet and then at Jack and me, his shaggy eyebrows raised. "Billy, you better hold onto this filly, she got spirit."

Jack said, "Don't pay no attention to Boone, Miss Harriet. He's got the manners of a shithouse rat."

At that Boone laughed out loud. Seemed like the worse things you said about him, the more he liked it. Anyway, from then on Boone and Jack were nice as pie to Harriet. Since she'd passed Boone's test of grit, he had nothing but good things to say about her. As we were leaving that afternoon, Boone and Jack invited Harriet to drink whiskey with us in the evening. "Put hair on your chest," he said, and then added, "Red hair." Harriet laughed and said that was the last place she wanted hair.

One time Harriet and I had a whole afternoon together. The ship was tied up for the day, so we bolted for a long walk to one of the abandoned Mandan villages. One reason for going, aside from the walk, was because of the story Jack Gallagher had told us the night before about the Mandans.

Jack said twenty-six years ago, in 1847, there were over four thousand Indians living there in the Mandan villages, mostly farmers growing corn and squash and beans and such. They were a trustful folk, and when the white men came to trade, the Mandans welcomed them as brothers. But the white men brought with them the gift of smallpox, and it wiped out nearly the whole tribe. "Maybe a hundred and fifty Indians left," he said, "lazin around the village."

What Harriet and I saw as we ambled through one of the villages was mostly old broken-down lodges, caved in from the roof, posts sticking up, beams lying on the ground, rafters in a heap. Some were burned out, with charred black posts still standing. We could tell the lodges had been large and sturdy at one time, thirty or forty feet across, but no more.

There were some Indians left in the village trading skins for whiskey, a few squaws offering sexual intercourse for trinkets, a couple mangy dogs running around, but the whole scene was so sorrowful, it'd make a grown man cry. Harriet said it was so wretched somebody ought to write a book about it. I said who'd want to read a book like that?

As we were trudging home late that afternoon, we came across something struck Harriet even harder than the Mandan village. In the distance but clear as day, we saw an Indian woman kneeling down on a high bank overlooking the river. Next to her was a platform raised up in the air and something lying on the platform. She was wailing and crying and carrying on like I'd never seen before, even slashing and cutting her arms and chest with a knife. This was so crazy I didn't know what to make of it, but Harriet did. She said the woman was mourning her dead husband lying up there on the platform.

We did a lotta walking and talking those last few days on the boat, but there was one night stood out from all the rest. It was near the end of the journey, the third night before landing at Fort Benton, and it was late, after Harriet's aunt had gone to bed, and the ship was quiet except for a few men drinking and talking on the deck. We located two deck chairs and sat side by side on the second deck looking out over the river and up into a sky swarming with stars. I'd brought some whiskey mixed with water in a canteen, and we sipped some while we talked. Just talking together was a joy.

I had thought before about sexual intercourse with Harriet but never brought it up because we hadn't even kissed yet. It was a well-known fact among us boys that you had to kiss a girl first before raising the subject of sexual intercourse.

Anyway, that night we did a lotta talking. I remember saying I didn't know what I was going to do after I finished working in the gold fields, although I wanted for sure to see my mother and sisters again.

Harriet said she was definitely going back to St. Louis after a year in Fort Benton, but once she got back, she didn't know what she was gonna do either. She'd daydreamed of maybe enrolling in one of those new normal colleges and teaching history in a secondary school. More kids were going to secondary schools now, and more teaching jobs were open to women. Either that, she said, or open up her own business. Not a dress shop, like most girls dreamed of, but a fur trading business. She might learn something about the fur trade at Fort Benton, so when she went back to St. Louis, she'd know how to do it.

We looked out over the tail end of the boat at the river, churned by our sidewheels, and we wondered how the moon, rising up on the horizon before us, could make such a straight path of light over the water not to anywhere else except right to us. Then we played a game of staring straight up at the stars as long as we could without blinking. We tried to guess how many stars there were—"Countless," she said—and how far away they were—"Millions of miles," I reckoned.

She said it made her dizzy to stare that long.

I said, "Makes me wish I could swerve and dodge through those stars on the wings of an eagle."

She smiled and said quietly, "Makes me think of poetry. 'Magic casements, opening on the foam of perilous seas, in faery lands forlorn.' That's John Keats."

I remembered the German professor in St. Louis and said, "Harriet, have you ever thought of the sky as being the face of God?"

She was silent, then repeated the words. "That's poetic, Billy, that's downright poetic. I've never heard such a thing before. My aunt once told me the stars were God's jewels which he scattered across the sky to decorate the heavens for folks like us to enjoy."

She reached over and took my hand in hers. Hers was warm and delicate, and I squeezed it. Squeezing it was my way of saying I liked her.

We were silent a long time after that, and finally she said we ought to go in, it must be at least three o'clock in the morning. It was a funny thing to say, because neither one of us was the least bit sleepy. But we got up and walked back to her cabin as if we were puppets on strings. At her door, standing in the shadow of the moon, I leaned forward to kiss her good night. Instead of pushing me away, she kissed back so hard it about took my hair off. We stood there looking in each other's eyes and agreed to meet the next day.

I didn't sleep that night. Lying out there on deck in the midst of a bunch of snoring men, ready to jump out of my skin, I thought about Harriet. She was pure girl the way she kissed and held my hand, the way I wanted to press against her, but she was also like a boy the way she liked to do adventurous things. She was Sara Belnap and Jack Coppedge all wrapped up in one person.

Next day I was standing at the railing waiting for her, when instead of Harriet her aunt appeared. She took my arm, walked me over to a place further down the railing where nobody could hear us, and said in a hard strong voice, "I never, ever want you to see my niece again!"

I was flabbergasted. "Why?" She said Harriet was all excited about some cockamamie story she'd heard from me about the sky being the face of God. As far as she, Mrs. Featherstone, was concerned, that was blasphemy. "Blasphemy," she repeated, "of the worst kind." I hadn't heard that word before, so I asked her what she meant by blasphemy. She was fit to be tied with that question. "Never mind," she hissed, "just don't go near Harriet again."

Well, you can imagine how Harriet took to that. She found me later that day and said she'd be damned if she was gonna pay any attention to an aunt stuck in ignorance and superstition. She couldn't see me that night, but the following night, the night before we were going to land at Fort Benton, she'd meet me on deck after her aunt went to bed.

It seemed a long time waiting for that last night with Harriet. I stomped around the deck for hours it seemed, even looked up a couple words in the dictionary (including *blasphemy*), talked with Boone and Jack but stayed away from our friend Al K. Hall.

We met just as she had suggested, after her aunt was in bed asleep, and we stood at the rail on the second deck. But right off the bat I could feel something was bothering Harriet.

I tried to raise her spirits by saying we might meet again in St. Louis. All we had to do was stay in touch by letter and see what happens.

She lit up to hear that and said "Yes, we oughta do that, Billy, stay in touch by letter."

Then she fell silent, and we stood for a long time just looking at the moon and sky and the banks of the river on either side. Along this part of the Missouri the banks turned into high cliffs on both sides, towering bluffs and pillars and turrets of stone silhouetted by moonlight against the night sky. The wind whined through the pillars and peaks, and dark shadows fell onto the river.

Then Harriet spoke in a wavering voice. She said if we were gonna be true friends, we had to be truthful with one another. She looked up with eyes crying for help. "Can I tell you something you promise not to tell anyone else?"

I nodded. "'Course."

"You won't hold it against me?"

"Nope."

Then she took my hand and pressed it against her belly. "Feel that?"

"Feel what? Only thing I feel is a little swelling there."

While holding my hand against her belly she said, "That's not just a swelling, Billy, it's a baby growing in there."

I couldn't believe my ears. A baby! She had a baby! She was nineteen years old, and she wasn't even married. I sputtered out, "How'd it happen?"

"It's an awful story, Billy and you don't want to hear the whole thing. The only thing you want—no, the only thing I need to tell you is, I'm gonna have a baby and give it to my aunt and uncle to raise. I couldn't be a true friend and hide that from you."

"But I want to know what happened," I said.

"All I can say is I didn't want it to happen. I mean I didn't even want to do it. I was forced to do it."

"Forced?"

"That's right. An older man forced me against my will."

"Who was he?"

"I can't say."

"Why can't you say? You said close friends tell each other everything."

"Because it's too awful."

"But I wanna know."

She looked at me with sad eyes and whispered, "It was my papa."

Neither one of us said anything for a long time.

"You still talkin to me, Billy?"

"Course I am. T'wasn't your fault. That's all that counts." But I felt weak in the stomach, and my words sounded hollow.

I spent the next hour telling her it didn't make any difference. If she had the grit to tell the truth, I ought to respect her. But it wasn't easy.

We kissed each other good-bye, and I promised to stay in touch by letter. I saw she was beginning to cry, so I hurried away before I did too.

Next day we got off the boat separately. I watched from a distance while her uncle met and hugged first her aunt and then her. I noticed Harriet glancing around a lot, but I just stayed off in the distance feeling like a skunk.

Then, without thinking, I took off at a gallop toward the three of them as they were walking away from the dock. Out of breath, I said, "Harriet, how can I write?"

She cried, "Just write in care of my uncle, Mr. Abraham Featherstone."

I turned and ran away.

PART II

BANNACK

Chapter Sixteen

THE THREE OF US RODE out of Fort Benton on the wagon road south to Bannack. The road reached out ahead of us so far, it seemed to go all the way to the horizon, running and twisting its way like a snake through the yellow grasses and green sage of the high plains. Not a soul in sight, either, just wide-open country. There was a bite of cold in the early morning air, but it didn't discomfit me after being cooped up on that steamboat for a month; just riding out there in that open space under a big dome of blue sky raised my spirits higher than corn in August.

We set a steady pace for ourselves across the flat, windy plains, then angled across the sweet-smelling grasses of the Deer Lodge Valley and followed a rocky horse trail over the snow-covered Continental Divide. It was cold up there, so we didn't tarry. We eased on down the trail into the Big Hole Valley and entered into a sight to behold: a gigantic stretch of yellow grassland with hazy blue mountains rising like boundaries on both sides. My eyes took in so much territory that it looked like a world without end. Also a world without a living creature in sight.

So I whistled and said, "If that don't make the prettiest picture I ever saw, I'll be a monkey's uncle."

Jack turned to me and said, "Hell, you are a monkey's uncle, Billy. Ain't you heard o' this fella Darwin?"

Boone spit tobacco juice and said, "I'd say this ride's hard on the ass but easy on the eyes."

'Course we didn't do this whole trip in one day. Took us four all told, and all the time we're riding I'm getting itchier and itchier to get out there and start digging for gold.

The trail came into Bannack from the north, and we stopped atop a ridge that gave us a wide view of the town and nearby hills. Boone, Jack, and me sat our horses a few minutes and just stared. It was early evening, and the rays from the western sun lit the hills in a golden brown while the town below was in the shade. Smoke rising from several chimneys put a blue haze in the air. The town wasn't much to look at, a patch of brown wood buildings strung out on a bench of land bordering a creek that gushed with spring runoff. I reckoned that was Grasshopper Creek, where gold had been discovered the summer before.

"Fifteen hundred people livin down there, would you believe it?" Jack said.

Boone shook his head. "Don't look big enough to hold no fifteen hundred."

"That's 'cause those miners are also livin in the hills," Jack added, pointing to where miners had dug holes into the lower slopes of the hills around the town. "They're dug in like prairie dogs."

I couldn't help thinking how different this country was from back home in Illinois. The hills back home were so thick with woods, you couldn't see the ground underneath, but here, although the ground was covered with sagebrush and bunch grass, the hills were wide open, so open they looked naked to me, with only a few juniper and pine trees clustered at the tops.

We eased our horses down the hill and into town, slouching along what I learned was Main Street past the Goodrich Hotel, Hoyt's Harness Shop, Le Grau's Bakery, and Crisman's General Store, where a big wagon train, with maybe twenty mules in front, stood outside being unloaded while some folks looked on. Boone made a beeline for the Elkhorn saloon—it had elk antlers over the front door—closely followed by Jack and me.

BANNACK

Respectable folks would call the Elkhorn a recruiting station for the army of drunks in Bannack. It was filled wall to wall with men in thick black beards, battered hats, and raggedy clothes, two deep at the bar and packed around tables. Wasn't a woman in sight except for a fat lady behind the bar. There was so much talk, it sounded like a hive of angry wasps, with shouts of laughter and profanity busting through the buzz. The reek of cheap whiskey and tobacco smoke and sweat made me dizzy for a second. One man at the bar couldn't find his mouth with a glass of whiskey he had in hand.

Boone took one deep draft of the smoke and sweat and whiskey, turned to Jack and me, and grinned ear to ear as if he'd just arrived in the promised land.

Standing behind the bar was a big man in a black hat with a narrow brim, long handlebar mustache, and tattoos in blue ink on both arms. One arm showed a sweet-looking mother holding her tiny baby, the other a naked gal with her back arched to show off her bare tits. Found out his name was Cyrus Skinner, and I soon learned he'd escaped from San Quentin prison two years earlier and, after chasing all over the Northwest, reckoned Bannack was the furthest from the law and civilization he could get.

"I reckon you boys new in town," Skinner said, laying his hands like slabs of meat on the counter. "There's so many no-goods like yourselves comin in, it's hard to keep track." When he smiled, the ends of his mustache turned up. "Cheapest whiskey we got is Valley Tan, made right here in Bannack for one dollar a bottle, the worst tastin stuff'll ever pass your lips."

It was, too. One slug, and I doubled over and couldn't breathe for a couple seconds. I found out the local boys called it "panther piss."

When a fella next to Boone said Bannack was the rowdiest town in the West, Boone shrugged and said, "Well, it just got rowdier." Then he drew his pistol and fired a shot into the ceiling. The whole saloon stopped talking, and in the silence Boone held up his glass of Valley Tan and shouted loud enough for the whole saloon to hear, "To Jefferson Davis, gentlemen."

One man sitting at a table nearby stood up and said, "Hell, I'll drink to that." Next thing I knew nearly half the saloon was on its feet giving a rebel yip and tossing down drinks in honor of the President of the Confederate States of America.

I was stupefied. Here I was up in the wilderness of the Northwest, far as a man could get from the war, and what do I find but a bunch of damn secessionists. I learned later these men came from states like Missouri, Tennessee, Kentucky, or Arkansas, most of them running away from something, the war or the law or the burden of a wife and kids, drawn away by the siren of gold.

Not everybody was a rebel, though. More than half the men wrinkled their faces in disgust, and one even jumped up and shouted, "And here's a drink to Abe Lincoln and the Union." A bunch of other men also stood up, and I stepped forward, and we all cried, "To the Union," and downed a slug of whiskey. The whole saloon suddenly went dead quiet: it was the quiet just before a big storm hit. A fellow in front of me was opening and closing his fists getting ready for a fight.

Then came a whack on the bar. Every head turned to see the fat lady standing there with a club in her hand yelling, "That's enough now, boys, git back to your drinkin." The spell broke, and everybody went back to drinking and talking.

Boone was chock-full of high spirits. He turned to the man next to him and slapped his back so hard the man's glass eye popped out and plunked down on the bar. I noticed the eye itself was painted lopsided on the glass, and the glass was getting yellow with age. The man shouted at Boone, "Now see what ya done? Goddammit, keep yer hands to yerself." He picked up the glass eye and stuck it back in his head.

I retreated into myself and watched while Boone talked with the gal behind the bar. She was a big woman, plump as a dry cow, with tits the size of muskmelons. Then Boone grabbed my arm and said, "You ain't met Nelly yet, Billy. She says there's a hurdy-gurdy place just down the street, and ten dollars gits ya a whole night o' furious fornication."

I shook my head and said I was going for some grub; my stomach was hurting.

Down the street at the Goodrich Hotel, I got a big plate of beans and bacon and thought, nossir, I was not going to get drunk, I was going for gold the very next day. So after eating I found a grassy spot under a big cottonwood down by the creek and threw out my saddle blanket and bedroll.

As I lay there, wrapped in my wool blanket and looking up through the branches of the cottonwood at the stars, I couldn't help thinking about the night on the steamboat when Harriet and me stared up at the stars together and held hands. She was so pretty with those lively blue eyes and thin curved lips like that actress, and so plucky, too, the way she stood up to everybody. I also thought of that swell in her belly and remembered touching it and seeing that scared look in her eyes. Damn if that didn't make me bite down. I'd write a letter, that much I could do, and I'd write to Mama too, soon as I got settled.

Chapter Seventeen

NEXT MORNING I TROOPED BACK to the Elkhorn saloon and found Boone and Jack asleep on two bunks attached to the wall in back. I woke them up, but Jack said, "Jesus Keerist, Billy, go by yourself you wanta go that bad."

So I stopped by Crisman's store and bought myself the cheapest little shovel and pan I could find and then set out hiking upstream east of town. Along the way I passed by claims already marked, where miners were working sluices they'd sunk into the creek, and trudged several miles further up the ravine till I found a spot that wasn't marked by a claim. I stood in the creek and dug down behind a boulder with the shovel and filled my pan, just like I was told to do.

I sloshed away everything in the pan till there was nothing left at the bottom. Then I filled the pan again and swirled the stuff around and dumped it out without getting a glimpse of anything looking like gold. I'd been doing this for an hour or so and trying a couple other spots along the creek when a miner happened by and said I was doing it all wrong. He showed me first how to fill the pan with rocks and gravel and dirt, then he held it under running water in the creek while he loosed everything with his fingers, separating all the rocks and dirt and sand. Then he tipped the pan forward slow and started washing everything out with a steady swirl. "Just remember, kid, the gold is heaviest." He swirled and sloshed away everything except the sand, and sure enough there it was, little gold bits mixed in with the black sand. He picked them out with his knife and dropped them into my outstretched hand.

"I'll be damned," I said. "How much this gold worth?"

He frowned, "Couple cents, maybe."

Anyway, after he left, I went back to work and still came up empty. The water was freezing cold, and my hands by this time were numb. But it didn't matter. It didn't matter because I was now in the grip of hope: every pan was another chance to get kissed by the goddess.

Then something happened. Nearby I saw a spot along a curve in the creek that looked real promising, dug down to bedrock just like I was supposed to, and dumped a shovel-full into my pan. I filled the pan with water and started swirling it around asking myself what I was doing wrong. As I watched the rocks and dirt swirl around in clumps, it struck me I wasn't separating things good enough. I raked my fingers through the rocks and gravel and dirt and sand until everything was plainly separated. Then I began shaking the rocks off first, then the gravel, then the dirt and finally, swirling at the bottom was the black sand—and there it was, by God, tiny glitters of gold against the black sand. That sight sent a shiver through me as strong as a kiss from Harriet.

The pieces were big enough I could pick them out with my fingers and put them into an empty box of chewing tobacco. By the end of the day I'd managed to stow a tiny pile of gold in my tobacco can.

In town I took the gold to Crisman's General Store, and George Crisman weighed it in the balance scales behind the counter. He said I had made the grand total of two dollars and sixty-five cents, which he would give me credit for if I wanted to buy something. So I bought a big can of sweet peaches right on the spot.

As I wandered over to find a grassy place along the creek to eat the peaches, I kept telling myself I'd done something mighty important that first day. I'd discovered gold. I'd made a little more in one day here in Bannack than I had in one day in the hospital in St. Louis.

Chapter Eighteen

THOSE HIGH SPIRITS AT FINDING gold the first day in Bannack didn't stay high very long. After two weeks of backbreaking work—wading in that freezing cold water, searching and digging and swishing and sifting over and over, hands colder than an icicle—I'd made a measly ten dollars. That was enough to get a room with another fella at the Goodrich Hotel and pay for three squares a day, but that was about all. It was no way to bring in a fortune.

To make matters worse, we had a lot of rain in those first two weeks, and when it rained in that high mountain country in June, it was damn cold, a lot colder than June in Illinois. So I took to going to the Elkhorn after work to get warm and cheered up. In fact, drinking was about the only way to get cheered up in that lonely country.

Anyway, on the last day of the second week there, feeling tired and wet and cold from the rain, I headed straight for the Elkhorn for a drink of panther piss. As I neared the saloon I saw the front door bust open and a whole bunch of fellas come staggering out. Two men in front of the crowd weaved and stumbled out into the street, which was now a patch of thick mud—gumbo, they called it. They had pistols on their hips and turned to face each other, hatless, ankle deep in the gumbo, rain running through their matted hair and down their faces.

"Pace it off, boys," someone from the crowd shouted, and when I looked, there was Boone Helm calling for those two fellas to start fighting.

The two men started walking away from each other until they got about twenty paces and then Boone cried, "Stop!" They turned and seemed scared to death by what they saw, because they started backing up further away from each other until they reached a place where I had to wonder if they were still within pistol range.

"That's far enough, goddammit," Boone cried. He lifted his own pistol, fired a shot in the air, and the two men went for their guns. But one fumbled and dropped his pistol in the mud and fell to his knees to fetch it while the other one fired. The man who had dropped his gun staggered to his feet amid a hail of gunfire and fired back. The gunshots created such a cloud of smoke in the wet air, the two men nearly disappeared from sight. Then the guns went silent and the smoke cleared, and the two of them were still on their feet, one with blood pouring down the side of his head, the other holding his left leg.

They holstered their pistols and slogged through the mud toward each other. The man with a mangled ear cried, "Good thing ya can't shoot worth a damn."

The other man, limping in the mud and grabbing at his left leg, said, "Shit, Ives, ya couldn't hit the ground with yer hat." When they got face to face, they busted out laughing. Throwing their arms around each other they slopped through the gumbo back into the saloon.

Well, that was my first witness of a gunfight, and it didn't look anything like what I'd read about in those penny dreadfuls. I supposed you'd call this one a draw.

Inside the saloon everyone was waving their hands and talking loud about the gunfight. I joined Boone and Jack at the bar and got a glass half full of whiskey from the bottle they had. While I was standing there, a young fella looking drunk came up and said, "Hey, there, pretty boy, I get the feelin you don't like Jefferson Davis. Least ya wasn't drinkin to him couple weeks ago."

I remembered this kid from the first night we came to town. Hoping he'd go away, I turned and put both elbows on the bar. But he grabbed and twisted me around by the shoulder to face him. "I'm askin ya a question, boy. Ya got somethin agin the Confederate States of America?"

I was scared to death but shrugged off his hand and said, "Get your snot-diggers off me, mister. I believe in the Union."

By this time Boone and Jack were staring at us. But instead of stopping things like I hoped they would, they just stood there watching. My knees were shaking, and I was scared shitless, but I had no choice. It was either stand up to this kid or get branded a coward.

So I walked out the front door of the saloon ahead of him, but no sooner was I outside than he stuck his foot between my legs and threw me forward off the boardwalk into the gumbo. Before I had a chance to get up, he jumped down and kicked me hard on the side of my face. I saw stars and grabbed my face to cover up while he kept kicking me. I rolled over several times real quick and jumped to my feet, and we stood there in the rain facing each other. I was covered with mud, and my eyes were blurred from the blood and water pouring into them. I held my head in my hands like I was too weak to fight, so when he stepped forward to finish me off, I surprised him by throwing a hard right smack to his left eye. He didn't fall down, but he staggered back, blood pouring from his eye.

We circled and threw wild punches at each other, sometimes connecting with glancing blows that didn't knock either of us down. By this time I wasn't scared; I didn't think about pain or hurt or anything, didn't even care about my life. I just hungered to hit him as hard as I could.

Then someone yelled, *"Stop it!"* We turned to see a man wearing a sheriff's badge and a brown slouch hat and clothes looking clean and neat. In a loud strong voice he said, "Everybody inside outta the rain!"

Inside the saloon the sheriff hauled me to one side and examined the cuts around my eyes. He took my hankerchief and pressed it against the wounds and told me to hold it there, and he'd be right back. I watched while he went to the bar and talked to the boy who'd started the fight. The boy nodded his head in a respectful manner, then turned and ambled out of the saloon holding his eye.

The sheriff walked over to a table where the two gunfighters were drinking whiskey. He stood with his hands on his hips and said something strong because they listened in silence, then they got up like puppets and followed him to the door of the saloon. I heard him say, "Now get your asses over there and get those cuts looked after by Doc Bissell."

The sheriff wasn't a big man, only about five feet seven inches tall and slender as a willow. He had a handsome clean-shaven face that stood out like a picture among the ugly faces and black beards in the saloon. Although he didn't look like a fighter, his eyes stared hard as steel, and his jaw was set in a way everyone took notice. He told me to come along home with him, and his wife'd fix me up.

Well, that was my first meeting with Henry Plummer. I had no idea then how dangerous his company was going to be in the months ahead. All I knew was I liked him right from the start.

We walked to his log home less than a block away, just off Main Street, not far from where Boone and Jack had their bedrolls cached under a wagon. His wife, Electa, sat up from her chair by the fireplace when we walked in and immediately clamped her hand to her mouth when she saw me. She was the prettiest girl I'd ever seen, prettier than Harriet anyway, although that wasn't saying a lot, since Harriet wasn't pretty unless you started talking to her. She wore a cotton dress of small red and white squares buttoned up to her chin, with her hair pulled back and tied tight behind.

"Oh, my" was the first thing she said. She took me over to a chair at the table and went to work fixing up my face, washing off all the blood and cleaning out the cuts and tying a bandage over one eye that went all around my head.

She'd already set the table except for the hot things she had on the stove. So soon as she finished fixing me up, she laid another place setting on the table, and we three sat down and plunged into a dinner of elk steaks, potatoes, and canned green beans. I hadn't eaten since lunch and ate like a starved man.

I couldn't help but notice that when the sheriff lifted off his brown slouch hat, which he wore low to his eyes, he had a long scar across the side of his head and forehead. His clean good looks made the disfigurement the more startling. I found out later he'd been cut in a whorehouse fight in Nevada City, California, and had shot to death the man who'd slashed him.

The sheriff asked me a lot of questions, and I was struck by how soft and easy he spoke and by his funny accent—turned out it was the way folks spoke in the state of Maine.

At the end of supper, he asked if I'd like to work on one of his claims. He had two good ones close to town and, since becoming sheriff, no longer had time to work them himself. He'd let me keep 75 percent of what I panned, and he'd take 25 percent. Another fella working for him, he said, was taking in ten dollars a day average, close to eight for himself.

Without even thinking, I said yes, I'd be much obliged. But later that night, when I was lying in bed thinking about things, I wondered what Boone and Jack would say, me working for a sheriff. Neither one had any use for sheriffs.

Chapter Nineteen

Turned out Boone and Jack didn't care a damn about me working for the sheriff. They were square in that way: they didn't want folks telling them what to do, and they didn't tell others what to do neither.

I worked hard that whole summer on the claims along Grasshopper Creek owned by Henry Plummer, mostly working with a pan but also setting a sluice by the creek bed and letting running water do some of the work for me. Most days I made a solid eight dollars, and that was after I set aside 25 percent for Henry. He took what I gave him without a word, which made me extra scrupulous in calculating his share.

My stake earned about 160 dollars a month, or nearly 500 dollars over the entire summer. 'Course, I didn't keep all that. My spending was so high I managed to save only a hundred of it. Thank God I cached it in Henry's safe at Crisman's store, otherwise I might not have saved even that much.

But the best thing that happened to me that summer—not counting the 500 dollars I made—was becoming a friend of Henry Plummer. Sometimes on Sunday, Henry hitched up his buggy, and he and Electa and I bumped along the road out of town for a picnic in the wilderness. I was never much for picnics myself, all that gazing around at the scenery and blabbing about the weather and the flowers and the rocks. I once heard a woman say, "Look there, honey, that's such a pretty rock." Can you beat that, a goddam rock!

Sometimes we rode over as far as the Big Hole Valley where the grassland reaches out flat for miles and Electa oohed and ahhed while Henry nodded in silence. He thought the big spaces made a person feel free, away from all the foolish conversation and people in town, and also it gave a person time to take stock. I couldn't argue with that.

One day he said, "You notice how everything looks pretty at a distance, Billy." He said a lot of things like that stuck like burrs in my head.

In general, though, Henry didn't say much, didn't shoot many arrows in the air, as they say. But when he let one go, it zingo hit the bull's-eye. One time I asked Henry to teach me to shoot a pistol, but he said "nope" in his even-tone voice; he didn't want to walk out in the street some day and see me with a gun on my hip. "A man carries a pistol long enough, it gets used," he said.

Sometimes we rode up to a mountain meadow that Electa especially favored, and she'd spread a picnic lunch on a blanket by a quiet pond. Things were greener in the meadow than on the hills, and the afternoon sun made the grass smell sweet and the earth feel warm. Some days the sun got so hot we took off our shoes and socks and waded in the pond.

Henry showed me how the beavers had made the meadow by gnawing down trees and damming up the creek. There were a lot of colorful wildflowers in the meadow too, and Electa always got a kick out of picking a bunch to take back with us. She tried to teach me to recognize the flowers, but I could never keep the names straight and didn't care anyway.

Electa usually brought a basket of food that included venison or elk steaks and potato salad and sometimes even a can of oysters, which she called a "delicacy" that only rich folk ate. Plus she nearly always made a peach pie that melted in your mouth, it was so delicious. I noticed that after we ate, Henry and Electa often stared and sighed at each other as if they had a fatal disease.

One day, while Henry was off in the woods somewhere, Electa told me how they met and fell in love. She said it happened on an experimental government farm up in Sun River, seventy-five miles from Fort Benton. She was living there with her sister, Martha Vail, her brother-in-law, James Vail, and their two children. James had signed a contract with the federal government to teach the Indians how to be farmers. "Civilize and Christianize the Indians" was the way the government put it. Never mind that the Indians didn't want to be Christian or civil or that they didn't want to be farmers.

Henry had been on his way back east to his home in Maine but missed the steamboat in Fort Benton. James Vail met Henry in one of the saloons in town and prevailed on him to come out to the farm to provide some protection from the Indians. It was pure coincidence he and Electa met. "Must have been God's will brought us together," she said.

The first night she saw Henry, she lost her common sense just looking at him, he was so handsome, and his voice was so strong and pure. Lucky for her, he felt the same way. He said she was pretty as a wildflower, and he'd never met a girl touched him as much as she had, a miracle in the desert. Two weeks after that first night he kissed her on the lips. They were standing on a high bench of land overlooking the prairie, and he took her hand in his, and after a few minutes just standing and looking out across the yellow plains, he tipped her chin up and kissed her. "I got tears in my eyes," she told me.

The next week he made an offer of marriage, saying she was the kind of woman that redeemed a man's life. He proposed he'd go down to Bannack where the gold strike had happened, and after making enough money for them to live together, he'd come back and fetch her. Then they'd get married.

Which is exactly what he did, except he came back as the sheriff of Bannack. The Methodist missionary, Reverend Reed, wasn't there so, Henry found a Catholic missionary named Father Minatre to perform the ceremony. Electa wore a modest brown calico dress, and Henry wore a blue suit foxed with buckskin. Three days later the two of them drove into Bannack on the buckboard of the ambulance wagon without a splinter of doubt they would live happily ever after.

Chapter Twenty

WHAT TO DO AFTER WORK at night was the prickliest thing of all.

'Course, there were Saturday night dances, but they weren't much fun because of the terrible scarcity of women in town. Out of the 1,500 folks in and around Bannack only about 150 of them were women, and most of them were the wives of the merchants and tradesmen. That meant the miners and roughs and lowlifes didn't have the taming influence of women to keep them in line.

I moseyed over anyway time to time. The dances were held in the same log building that was used for a church. One night I was standing with a bunch of men on a side of the dance floor opposite the women and girls on the other, and a grizzled old miner came up and said, "C'mon out here, boy, and shake a leg." Although I always thought it looked stupid two men dancing together, before I could say no, this old buggar had jerked me out on the floor, and with his arm around my waist, and while two fiddles, a banjo, and a tambourine sounded a quadrille, he and I bounced and slid and stumbled around the floor like a couple of damn fools.

This little miner had got himself all dressed up in a white shirt and black trousers, trimmed his beard, and slicked back his hair. In the middle of the dance, he said, "You're a good-lookin boy. I bet you got a good-lookin pecker too." Till then I'd just been feeling foolish, but now I got downright discomfited. He kept right on pumping my arm up and down and pulling me around the floor and then said he had some brand-new store-bought whiskey from Salt Lake City hidden outside, and if I came out with him he'd give me a slug of it. He smiled and whispered in my ear, "I'll show ya my pecker, too, you want to see it."

That was my last dance in Bannack.

Jacking off was a way to let off steam, I suppose, but that didn't take much time off the clock, figuring three or four minutes a whack.

Some nights I wrote letters to Mama and Harriet. Harriet wrote me and said she was fine and was gonna to have her baby in December. She said she'd probably go back to St. Louis sometime after the first of the year, leaving the baby with her aunt and uncle.

In my letter to Mama I said everything was just fine and not to worry, I was making money hand over fist. She wrote back saying how much she missed me. She also said that after I left, she didn't talk to Pa for a month. She told him if he didn't apologize for what he'd done to me, she'd never talk to him again. I guess he stewed over that and finally came out and said he'd apologize when I got back. She wished I'd come back soon just so she could hear him apologize.

Another thing I did at night was read a few books. A small library had opened in town, and Electa gave me a story by Edgar Allen Poe called *The Tell-Tale Heart* that was the scariest thing I ever read. Another she gave me was called *The Last of the Mohicans* by James Fenimore Cooper, and I liked that a lot. The owner of Goodrich also gave me a bunch of penny dreadfuls, such as *Varney the Vampire or The Feast of Blood*, *The Demon Barber*, *The Horror of Zindorf Castle*, *Wagner the Werewolf*, and *The Fatal Bullet*. I liked them, too, but they didn't stick like the harder books.

But the only trustworthy place to escape being lonely and get relief from the boredom was at the Elhorn saloon.

Cyrus Skinner invented a game that summer which aimed to see who could stand on a plank the longest while drinking whiskey from the bottle. I was there the night Boone and Jack tried it. They joined four other men on the plank so there were six men standing in a row facing the crowd in the saloon. Skinner gave each man a bottle of Valley Tan and said whoever finished the bottle and was still on the plank won the contest. If more than one person was standing, he'd give them another bottle.

The winner got a free bottle of Valley Tan.

Naturally, everyone in the saloon bet on who'd stick the plank longest. All six men stood in plain view while the bets were made. The fella next to me allowed as this was Western theater at its finest, better than Shakespeare.

After the men on the plank got to drinking, fellas in the crowd started yelling to make them laugh and fall off. "Hey, Red," one fella at our table shouted, "I hear ya got shit for brains."

Another fella, known for his ability to fart any time he wanted, jumped up and shouted, "Yer time's up, all o' ya!" The he extended his hand like a pistol and fired off a fart. I laughed so hard I shed tears.

The men on the plank laughed too, but nobody fell off. The first man to go was the miner with a glass eye. About half his bottle drunk, he tipped his head back for another gulp and kept right on going backward till he hit the floor flat on his back. I couldn't see whether his eye came out or not. 'Course the crowd roared. I heard the old bugger never woke till next noon. Another man on the plank saw Red topple over backward and got to laughing so hard he couldn't stop, started to double up tighter and tighter till he just rolled over frontwards and hit the floor head first.

Jack went down fourth after finishing more than three quarters of the bottle, and he never spoke again that night. Finally there were two left, Boone and another fella, and the other fella finally took a drink and just stepped off the plank and fell onto a table in front of him. The boys at the table slapped him on the back and pushed him over onto the floor.

Boone finished his bottle while still on the plank and then looked around grinning, weaving like he was the cat's pajamas. Everybody clapped and hooted.

Another twist off this game was to see how long a man could just stand on the plank, drink or no drink. The record was seven hours. Skinner offered a hundred dollars to anyone who could break the record. From the very beginning Jack Gallagher talked about breaking the record, saying he'd work seven hours and one minute for a hundred dollars any day. Hell, that was good pay.

Eventually he did, too, when he was broke, but you can imagine how much fun it was watching a man stand seven hours and one minute on a plank.

Those games of Cyrus's took your mind off the loneliness. But the biggest user of time by far was gambling. Those miners were gamblers by nature anyway, and the lack of things to do just made it worse. For instance, Skinner put two cubes of sugar on the bar and took bets from everyone on which cube a fly'd land on first. When a fly landed on one of the cubes, half the bar would cheer and the other half moan. One time I started betting a dollar a throw on the flies, and before I knew it, I'd lost five dollars.

Cards were the big thing, though. I learned to play poker decently well, although over the summer I probably lost close to a hundred dollars. The only time I seemed to win was when I played with those boys who were drunk and careless. Which I did whenever I could.

One night I was in the Elkhorn playing stud poker with a bunch that included a professional card sharp called Banfield and a miner named Sapp. Banfield was winning most hands, and Sapp was losing. Sapp suspicioned the card sharp was cheating, and so he watched with a careful eye till finally he saw the sharpie draw a diamond off the bottom to fill a flush. "I saw that, Banfield," he cried, pointing to the card. Banfield jumped up madder than hell and drew his pistol.

Someone yelled, "Wait a second there, Banfield, he ain't even heeled."

Sapp held his hands in the air to show he wasn't armed. Banfield gritted his teeth awhile and then sat back down and said, "Ya talk like that agin, mister, and I'll blow your head off whether you're heeled or not."

After playing a spell, Sapp seemed to forget Banfield's warning because he suddenly blurted out, "I think ye're a goddam cheat, Banfield."

This time Banfield drew his pistol and fired. Sapp ducked behind a post just before Banfield pulled the trigger, so he escaped being hit. Meantime, Doc Bissell, who was standing at the bar, threw Sapp his pistol to square the fight. Banfield fired again, and Sapp fired back, and the both of them started weaving and firing and ducking from post to post while all the rest of us flopped and scrambled on the floor.

When their guns clicked empty, both men were still standing untouched. They tossed their guns away and started throwing fists, but several of us jumped up from the floor and pulled them apart, yelling to stop it, goddam, stop it. When things quieted down, we heard a moan and looked under the gambling table, and there was the dog named Toodles, dying from a gunshot wound. Everyone gathered around Toodles, saying what a shame it was, when someone else from the back of the saloon called out that Carrhart had been shot. George Carrhart was a man known for having once been a member of the California Legislature until John Barleycorn got the best of him. He had been sleeping in one of the bunks in back and took a stray bullet to the head, killing him instantly.

Two of Carrhart's friends looked at the body and got so damn mad they drew their pistols and searched around for Banfield and Sapp. But Banfield and Sapp had seen them draw and were hell-bent for the door. The two men fired, hitting Banfield in the finger and Sapp in the leg, but they made it out the door anyway. Poor Sapp didn't take care of the wound in his leg and died of infection two weeks later.

So it went.

The trouble for me was, I couldn't drink like Boone and Jack. A few glasses of whiskey, and my head started spinning as if I'd just stepped off the merry-go-round at the state fair. Many a night I staggered back to the Goodrich and lay there in bed while the room tipped and whirled around me. Usually I'd feel better if I just got up and puked out the window. Then the next day I'd struggle to work with a mouth so dry I couldn't spit and a raging case of the shits. You'd think that'd be enough to make a fella stop, wouldn't you? Ha!

Chapter Twenty-One

THEN SOMETHING TERRIBLE HAPPENED AT the end of the summer: a miner named John Horan killed his partner, Harrison Keeler. Henry felt chagrined about it for two reasons: one, because he knew and liked the two men and thought it was a damn shame, and second, because he was proud so little crime was happening in Bannack that summer.

Henry claimed that if you took away all the drinking and carousing and fighting in the saloons, Bannack was no worse or better than any other town its size in the States. Those drunken miners and lowlifes in the saloons might be offensive to the churchgoing folks in town, but the truth was they weren't robbing and killing folks, they mostly just hurt themselves.

He said there had been only three robberies all that summer in Bannack. The first one happened to Mr. and Mrs. Davenport who got robbed while eating their lunch on Rattlesnake Creek. But the thief must have had a guilty conscience, because the following week he left Mrs. Davenport's money under the door of her cabin. A second robbery happened at the house of a Frenchman named Le Grau who was both the baker and blacksmith. Lucky for Le Grau, though, the thieves only got a couple o' dollars. The third robbery was of Dutch Fred who folks said was so dumb he deserved to be robbed. Nobody could figure out how much Dutch Fred lost because he kept saying different things according to how drunk he was.

Most of the trouble happened, Henry said, when disputes flared up between miners over claims. Henry had a way of quieting those men down by his common sense and personal authority that left many saying he was the best sheriff they ever saw. Cyrus Skinner said Henry's secret was making one fella stand in another fella's shoes for a minute, just to see what it looked like from the other side. Then sometimes Henry would pretend to be dumber than he was, just to get the folks to loosen up and listen. I wished my pa was more like Henry.

Anyway, Horan killed Keeler even though the two men shared a cabin and were best friends. One day they got into an argument over who was supposed to cook breakfast, and the words got so hot, Horan lost his head and shot Keeler dead.

Horan turned himself in to Henry, and Henry locked him up in the town jail. The merchants had been yelling all summer for a jail but refused to pay any taxes to build one. It got done finally 'cause the miners and roughs, the folks most likely to use it, chipped in enough to build it.

Anyway, Horan told Henry he shot Keeler because the sonofabitch wouldn't stop talking, just kept going on and on while he, Horan, couldn't get a word in edgewise. Finally Horan reached the end of his rope; he fired three loads into him while Keeler kept right on spouting words. It wasn't till the last shot Keeler stopped talking, opened his eyes wide, and dropped dead.

This happened on a Sunday morning. I was still in my room at the Goodrich when someone yelled up the news. All I had to do was come downstairs to see Keeler stretched out in the lobby with his eyes still open in a state of eternal surprise. When Henry came in, he closed the man's eyes.

A miners court was held out in the open air under the supervision of Judge Ray Hoyt. Horan took the witness stand and said he was sorry. Keeler was his best friend, and he didn't mean to do it. He begged for mercy.

The jury found him guilty, and Judge Hoyt said, "Don't have much choice here, John. I'm sorry to say the law demands you be hanged."

BANNACK

Henry told his deputies, Buck Stinson and Ned Ray, to get a gallows built that day for use the next. Then he went to Judge Hoyt and pleaded to commute Horan's sentence to banishment. But Hoyt said he couldn't do it because the crime was murder, and he was getting leaned on pretty heavy by the new territorial Supreme Court Judge Sidney Edgerton and a young lawyer named Wilbur Sanders, his nephew, both just arrived in Bannack. They said hanging was the law for that crime, no getting around it, and besides, it was necessary to set an example to others who might be thinking along the same lines as Horan.

Henry said there was no lesson to others because no others were thinking along the same lines, but it didn't do any good.

The night before the hanging, a man named X Beidler stopped the sheriff on the street and said he'd hang Horan free of charge if Henry wanted him to. Beidler was a short, stocky man whose round, bald head sat on his shoulders like a cannonball, and he had the reputation of being the most righteous and the cruelest man in the territory, a man who liked to hurt people. Henry told him in a voice tighter than usual to get the shit out of his way.

A crowd of nine hundred people showed up for the hanging. I stood right near the new gallows, two upright logs connected by a crossbeam at the top, and watched while Henry walked up under the crossbeam holding Horan's arm hard against his side to keep the poor fella from collapsing. I heard Henry say he was sorry to do it, but there was nothing he could do.

Horan stumbled and said, "I reckon it ain't your fault, Henry."

When Stinson helped him onto a wooden crate and slipped the noose around his neck, Horan had tears steaming down his face. Henry asked if he had anything he wanted to say for his last words. At first Horan shook his head. Then he looked over at sheriff and said, "Life's a bowl a shit, Henry."

Chapter Twenty-Two

MY FIRST GOOD LOOK AT Wilbur Sanders—aside from seeing him in the crowd at the hanging—was the place you'd least expect to see a man like Wilbur Sanders, at the Elkhorn saloon. It was a Sunday afternoon, and the place was filled with the usual lowlifes trying to drink off their hangovers.

I was feeling pretty shaky myself, sitting at a table with Boone and Jack, Haze Lyons, a Mexican named Joe Pizanthia, and a cook called Red Yeager. Yeager's fingers were shaking so hard, he couldn't get a glass a whiskey to his mouth. He had failed several times and was just sitting there staring helplessly at the glass.

I was watching to see what Red was going to do next. He was so shaky his lips trembled and the hair of his red beard quivered. Finally Red took his long, dirty red hankerchief and looped it around his neck in back and pulled it tight, holding both ends in front of him. Then with one hand he held tight the whiskey glass, and with the other hand he began to pull the end of the hanky like a pulley, so the glass was hoisted to his mouth without spilling the whiskey.

Boone looked at him and shook his head. "You been seein any snakes lately, Red?"

Red finished the whiskey, then said, "I'll be steady in a minute, boys, you pour me another glass o' that Barleycorn there."

Jack Gallagher looked at him and said, "You'll be steady, all right, you'll be so steady you can't move." Everyone laughed except Red who was wringing his hands to get the shakes out.

Joe Pizanthia, who was called the Greaser, poured Red another glass of whiskey. Joe spoke with a Mexican accent but hardly ever said a word.

Haze Lyons said, "I've been thinking of George Carrhart lately, boys. You think he's roastin in hell? He surely did enough evil things to qualify himself." Haze Lyons was educated at an eastern college called Yale and came out west after getting into a bad scrape with the law.

"He ain't playin no harp in heaven," Jack said. Jack was wearing a Confederate cavalry hat and coat he'd picked up in Salt Lake City, and the hat, which had a feather in it, was tilted to one side.

"I'll betcha old George's mighty thirsty right now," Red Yeager said, his hands still shaking. He cackled and showed a broken row of black teeth. "I expect there's no whiskey in hell."

"No whiskey in heaven either, you dumb shit," Haze Lyons said.

Red stared at him and smiled. "Then I ain't goin to neither place."

"Neither place'd take ya."

"Ain't no such place as hell," Boone Helm said. He took off his hat and ran his fingers though his tangled, greasy hair. "Preachers talk about hell to keep folks in line."

"Sure as hell didn't keep you in line," Jack said.

"Shit, best thing about you is that Confederate coat," Boone muttered.

Haze Lyons said, "I believe in hell. How else the wicked gonna get punished?"

"They ain't," Boone said.

"I believe in this fella Darwin," Jack said. "This fella Darwin says we're all descended from the apes, and I say hell yes we are, just look over there at Cyrus Skinner, and tell me we ain't descended from the apes."

Haze Lyons said, "I danced with a gal last night looked like she was descended from the apes."

Then, before I got a chance to say I believed in hell, Wilbur Sanders appeared right out of the blue standing just inside the door. And he was a mighty imposing figure in his black frock coat and white shirt and tie and wide-brimmed hat pulled down to his eyes.

He had a neatly trimmed black beard and a rock-solid face. Seemed like everybody in the saloon stopped talking at the same time.

"I've got something to say to you boys, and I'm going to say it quick." He looked around shooting bullets with his eyes. "My wife Hattie was out shopping the second day we arrived in town, and she heard the dirtiest, foulest, most unchristian language she's ever heard in her life. Right outside here, on the public boardwalk. She's afraid to take the children out of the house for fear they'll hear more of that same execrable talk. So I'm telling you right now to stop it! Stop your cursing and swearing and insulting remarks in front of the women and children of this town."

His words were strong and clear and rushed out without a hitch. I had never heard the word *execrable* before, but I sat there flabbergasted by the man's nerve, walking into the Elkhorn by himself and delivering a sermon to the worst roughs in town. Had to respect him for that.

That wasn't all, either. After looking around with a deadly stare, he said, "I also want to remind everyone here that this town is part of the union of the United States of America. If I hear any more seditious talk, I'm going to the law about it. There's no place for traitors in Bannack. If you have any sense, you'll pay heed to what I say."

Nobody took a breath. I thought sure Boone would shout something, but he was flabbergasted too. Besides, Wilbur Sanders didn't leave any time for discussion. Soon as he finished his last word, he turned on his polished black boots and strode out like his majesty, the King of France.

For about five seconds the whole saloon was silent. Then everybody started talking. Boone flung his hat to the floor with a whack. "Listen to me, boys, I know somethin about that sonofabitch. He's a teetotalin Methodist Yankee lawyer." Boone hawked a gob on the floor. "Ya can't get no worse than that," he said, holding up three fingers. "Temperance, Methodist, and Yankee."

Haze Lyons said, "I saw him puttin up a Union flag outside the new judge's cabin over in Yankee Flat."

"He did that?" Boone cried. "Goddamn if that ain't an insult to every man sittin at this table."

It wasn't an insult to me, and I started to feel discomfited by the way things were going. Boone didn't look at me. He glanced over at Jack and said, "Ya still got that Confederate flag in yer saddlebag, Jack?"

Jack came back a few minutes later and spread out the flag. Boone said, "I say let's show the colors to the new folks in town."

Half the saloon followed Boone outside. He tied the flag to his rifle and untied his horse from the hitching rail. "C'mon, boys," he said as he mounted up.

Half a dozen other fellas fetched their horses and rode up next to him while he waited. When everyone was ready, he yelled, "Let's go, boys," and the whole bunch thundered hell-bent up and down Main Street, Boone holding the flag high in one hand and cutting loose a rebel yip. He thundered back to the Elkhorn and handed the flag to a young fella slouching on the boardwalk and shouted, "Stand at attention when you hold that flag, boy."

Boone pulled the horse up tight, dug in his heels, and then let go, and the beast bolted off at a gallop into the street and across the small log bridge that led from Main Street to the residential area called Yankee Flat. He stormed up to the cabin occupied by the new supreme court judge, Sidney Edgerton, leaped off his horse, and tore down the American flag that was flying over the yard.

He scrambled onto his mount and, flag in hand, galloped back across the bridge with a loud clatter and up to the Elkhorn. Outside the saloon he laid the American flag across a hitching rail and lit the corners with a match. While the flag burned, Boone and a bunch of others sang a chorus of "Dixie."

By this time I was long gone, watching from in front of the Goodrich Hotel up the street. What I saw riled my guts, and I decided on the spot I was through being friends with Boone and Jack. It was one thing putting up with them being lazy and drunk, but another putting up with traitors.

Chapter Twenty-Three

Next time I saw Wilbur Sanders was in the sheriff's office at the back of Crisman's store. I'd taken the afternoon off at Henry's invite to watch the race that afternoon between Fast Jim Hatch and Daly's mule. Just before we got up to head for the race, Wilbur Sanders strode in looking fit to be tied.

But he took one look at the sheriff, and that stern look just plumb disappeared. Made me recall one woman saying Henry's looks were so fine there was something feminine about him. Whatever it was, the icy look on Sanders's face melted away when he saw Henry.

Thrusting out his hand, he said, "Wilbur Sanders, Sheriff. Folks like to call me Colonel Sanders, but you're at liberty to call me Wilbur if you prefer." He gripped Henry's hand hard. The two men stood looking at each other longer than usual, Henry clean-shaven, Sanders's black beard neatly trimmed. The colonel said, "I've heard good reports about your tenure in this town, Sheriff. Makes me think we can work together to make Bannack an even better place to attract new immigrants." He glanced over at me sitting in a straight chair against the wall and said, "I saw you in the Elkhorn the other day, young man. That's no place for a boy like you."

I had to smile. I liked the way he didn't hold back what he thought, just shoved the words out there, come hell or high water.

Henry had on his slouch hat—I believe he liked to hide that ugly scar of his—denim trousers, and a loose flannel shirt, his easy dress matching his easy manner. Wilbur Sanders, on the other hand, wore a black frock coat, white shirt and tie, and high-crowned black hat, dressed to fit his manner. He was a mite taller than Henry and stood straighter, his shoulders square as a ruler, his chin raised higher. When he took off his hat, I noticed his hair was already getting sparse in front even though he was only twenty-nine, a year younger than Henry.

Colonel Sanders didn't offer to shake hands with me. He just sat down on the other chair next to the cast iron stove in Henry's small office and started to explain why he was there, namely because the American flag had been torn down and burned by a bunch of seccessionists, and he wanted the rebels brought to justice. "Burning the flag is a crime and a desecration," he said. Being around Sanders had me running to the dictionary Mrs. Rhinehart gave me, this time for the word *desecration*.

Colonel Sanders also thought Henry ought to know something about who he, Colonel Sanders, was, since he would be in the position of advising him from time to time. Henry smiled at this and suggested he tell us all about himself on the way to the race just south of town.

So off we went down Main Street, Sanders on his roan gelding, Henry on his red sorrel (best-looking horse in town), me on the gray nag I'd bought for thirty dollars. We rode out along the wagon road about five minutes and ascended a slight rise from where we could see the whole race. The race course, Henry pointed out, was simply the wagon road that ran parallel to the creek. The racers ran out about a quarter mile, turned and came back the same road to the starting line. At the starting line it looked like about five hundred men mixing together. Not a single woman.

There wasn't a cloud in the sky that September day, just pure blue, the sun throwing off such a hard light it made your eyes squint. Couldn't ask for a better race day. The grassy land around us was a golden brown except along the creek where the leaves of the cottonwoods were turning yellow and orange and the bushes were blood red.

Henry commenced to explain how the race came about. Jim Hatch ran so fast, his friends bragged that with a little head start he could beat Daly's mule in a race. That got folks talking and arguing so much, Cyrus Skinner stepped in and worked out a deal where they'd run a half-mile race, but Jim got a fair head start. Skinner then took bets and declared half the pot went to the winner of the race, half to the bettors.

While we were waiting for the race to begin, Colonel Sanders told all about himself. He said he was there in Bannack to establish his own law practice and become a leader of the community; he was also there to assist his uncle, Sidney Edgerton, to get a new territory established in what was now Idaho Territory. Henry and I both looked surprised to hear that. Sanders said, "You heard right, a brand new territory." He said Sidney Edgerton was somebody the sheriff better get to know, because Sidney was more than likely going to be the governor of the new territory. Bannack would be the capital.

Henry said that was interesting, and he'd like to know how he was going to do that. By this time Fast Jim had walked ahead to his place further up the road, and Daly was sitting his mule at the starting line. We kept an eye on the race while listening to Sanders ramble on.

The colonel didn't even notice the race, he just kept talking. He said Sidney Edgerton had been a Republican Congressman from Ohio a few years back and recently had been appointed by Abraham Lincoln as a Supreme Court Judge for the entire Idaho Territory. Edgerton and his family and Sanders and his family had been on their way to Lewiston, the capital of the territory, but when they got to Bannack, they recognized right away the territory was too big to govern from Lewiston. All these new mining camps and settlements sprouting up in eastern Idaho were too far away from the capital. What was needed, they saw right away, was to carve out a new territory. So they were staying in Bannack and making plans. Soon as they had a good solid case prepared, they were going to Washington to present it before Congress.

I noticed the Colonel had a funny way of not looking at either Henry or me when he spouted his fine words. He just stared straight out as if he was making a speech. What he said was interesting, but he kept blabbing away about other things even after the race began. So we had to listen to Sanders blab at the same time our eyes were glued to the race between Fast Jim and Daly on his mule.

I could see Jim Hatch had jumped off to a wide lead before Daly got his mule into full stride. But I could also see that the lead wasn't going to hold for long. Although Jim was running like a deer, the mule was faster and steadily closing ground. By the time they reached the turn and started back down along the creek, Jim had lost a good bit of his lead. I felt my heart starting to pound. I hadn't reckoned how much I wanted Jim to win.

Meantime Sanders kept right on blabbing. Now he was speaking about Boone Helm and his bunch of rebels burning the American flag again. He called it a crime committed by treasonous men bent on overthrowing the order and authority of the Union. It was also a betrayal of the founding fathers and an affront (his exact word) to our soldiers dying on the battlefields.

"Wait a minute!" Henry said curtly. "Looks like this race is gonna be close."

I glanced at Sanders in time to see his face turn red as the branches of those bushes along the creek, the muscles in his cheeks twitching from clenching his teeth. But he said nothing in reply.

We sat our horses in silence, watching the distance close between Fast Jim and the mule. I gritted my teeth, as Daly was whipping the beast and it looked like Jim was starting to falter. The finish line was coming up fast, and I thought sure the mule was pounding over the ground fast enough to overtake the man. Then Jim glanced back and saw the mule closing, and it seemed to give him a terrible fright because he gave a final spurt of speed right before the finish line. The crowd was shouting and screaming, and the hooves of the mule were thundering in the air as Jim flung his body across the finish line a splinter ahead of the mule.

As we walked our horses back to town, Sanders didn't speak, but I could see his mood had changed. Finally, just before we got back to Crisman's store, he asked Henry between gritted teeth what he was going do about Boone Helm and his renegades burning the flag.

Swinging down from his horse, Henry said he'd already talked to Boone about it, told him he had a choice of either promising never to do that again or being banished from Bannack, one or the other. Boone had promised he'd never do it again, so Henry felt that was all he could do considering the way the sentiments of the people in town were so divided on the war.

Colonel Sanders looked shocked. As the three of us strode back into Crisman's store, Sanders said, "Why, that's a travesty, Sheriff." (Another one of those words.)

Henry just shrugged and said, "You don't seem to understand, Colonel. Half this town is in accord with Boone Helm. I arrest Boone, we have a war on our hands. I've made sure this won't happen again, that's all."

There was a long silence while we made our way past the shirts and pants and socks and hankies for sale in Crisman's store to Henry's office at the back. I started talking about the race, saying how great it was Jim beat the mule, but I could see the colonel's forehead was wrinkled; he was waiting to say more. Finally he said, "You're wrong, Sheriff, just plain wrong. You don't seem to realize we're fighting a war in this country. There's no running away from that."

Henry shrugged. "I'm not runnin," he said strongly, "I'm preservin the peace. What would you do?"

"First, I'd throw them in jail. Then I'd convene a miners court to consider either hanging or banishment."

Henry shook his head. "No miners court would hear the case, Colonel."

Sanders clenched his jaw and shot back, "Then get a citizens group to help you. I heard of a town in the Southwest where citizens got together and kicked the no-good rebels and drunks and renegades out. Just kicked them out of town."

Henry raised his eyebrows. "On what grounds?"

"On what grounds? On being enemies of the community, vagabonds, traitors." The colonel's voice was loud enough now, I was sure the folks in the front of the store could hear him.

Henry stared at Wilbur Sanders real hard. "I'm stickin by the miners code of law."

"You call this miners system of justice *law*. That's one good reason we need to establish a new territory out here, a good system of law."

"The miners code is the law that got me elected sheriff," Henry said, his voice hard now and his eyes cold, "and it's the law I stand to enforce."

Henry turned to me and said, "You can go if you want to, Billy." I shook my head and said it was all right, I was interested in what they were saying. Henry laughed, and Sanders glanced over and said, "Stay out of that Elkhorn saloon, young man."

Henry rose and said he'd think about what the colonel was saying, but he wasn't going to arrest anybody, and that was final. The colonel got up and instead of shaking hands said something that really took me by surprise. He said, "Before I came to see you today, Sheriff, I heard about your violent past, but I told myself to hold up judgment, a lot of folks think you're doing a good job. What I find is someone who can't seem to make up his mind which side he's on in this war." He compressed his lips. "Just don't say I didn't warn you."

Henry didn't show any emotion in his face, but his gaze was deadly cold and hard. He wasn't thinking kindly thoughts of Colonel Sanders.

Anyway, that was the end of the conversation.

Later that night I lay in bed thinking Wilbur Sanders and Henry Plummer were a pair of contraries if there ever were such things. Henry had a "live and let live" view of life, but Wilbur was a "behave like you're supposed to or else" kind of person. It crossed my mind that Colonel Sanders was more like my pa and Henry more like my mama. I knew in my bones that something bad was going to happen between those two.

Chapter Twenty-Four

What Wilbur Sanders said about Henry's past, his "violent" past, stuck like a splinter in my mind. I was curious. Henry didn't seem like a violent man to me; just the opposite, in fact. But I didn't know much about him neither. All I knew was, he didn't like to talk about himself. Once he told me, "My pa said there was no need to get stuck in the past; it's the wrong place to live." So I didn't bother to ask him. Instead I nosed around till I heard of someone who didn't have much backbone but was trustworthy with the truth and had been there in Bannack as long as Henry had. That man was a merchant named Francis Thompson, who ran his own dry goods store.

One morning I saw Thompson unloading a wagon, and I walked over and pitched in, carrying crates and boxes into his store. Thompson was much obliged, and when we finished, I asked him to tell me something about Henry Plummer, how he got to be sheriff, for instance. Thompson gave me a bottle of root beer, put his hand on my shoulder, and steered me out in back of the store. We sat down under a cottonwood by the creek, and he told me how Henry came to be sheriff.

Henry had ridden into town in the fall of last year with a no-good fella named Jack Cleveland. They had both been working on the government farm near Fort Benton where Henry met Electa.

BANNACK

Cleveland hated Henry's guts because Electa paid him no heed; all her attention went to Henry.

Once they arrived in Bannack, they went in opposite ways. Henry set himself hard to work to make enough money to get married and bring Electa back to live in Bannack. Wasn't long till folks grew to like and respect Henry, especially the miners, because he was smart and honest and always ready to help a person out.

Cleveland, on the other hand, was a bully, the kind of no-good who beat up on fellas smaller and weaker than himself. Worst than that, most folks also thought he was a thief and murderer. Although nobody could prove it, folks were pretty sure Cleveland had killed a miner named George Evans. Their reason was Cleveland, who was always broke, came into the Elkhorn flush with money one night and got drunk for three days. A week later someone found the body of Evans murdered and robbed right where Cleveland had last been with him.

All through the fall and winter Cleveland nursed his grudge against Henry, and finally it busted out one rainy night near the end of March in the Goodrich saloon. Henry was sitting at a table near the woodstove with several other fellas when a man named Jeff Perkins came over and told him Cleveland was snarling drunk and claiming Henry was his "meat" that night.

Hearing this, Henry shook his head in disgust. Last thing he wanted was a gunfight, but he'd hardly had time to think about it before Jack Cleveland staggered through the front door. His broad-brimmed hat was pushed back on his head, and his hair was sticking out all over. He swaggered over to the bar and slammed his hat down and said loud enough for everybody to hear, "I'm the chief in this here town, and nobody better say otherwise."

Henry saw him and said, "He looks like a gorilla talkin to itself."

Pretty soon the gorilla came over to where Henry and the others were sitting and said, "Ya still on that high horse o' yers, Henry? Ya never used to be so damned uppity."

Henry threw him a look and said, "Better leave, Jack, before you get yourself killed." Even though Henry had a quiet voice and a clean smooth face, he also had a cold, gray stare that'd make a grizzly think twice.

Instead of answering, Cleveland turned away and began cussing Jeff Perkins about some money he claimed Jeff owed him. Perkins denied owing him money, but Cleveland got louder and hotter till finally Henry got mad. "That's enough, Jack, he don't owe you nothing, and you know it."

The two men stared at each other a long minute, and then when Henry saw a flicker in Cleveland's eye, he went for his pistol. Although Cleveland made the first move, he didn't have a chance. Folks later said Henry was the fastest man in the whole territory; he could fire five loads in three seconds. His first shot hit Cleveland in the hip and knocked him to the floor, where he looked up and cried, "Ya wouldn't kill a man when he's down, would ya, Henry?"

"Get up!" Henry cried. Cleveland started to get up but made the mistake of raising his pistol at the same time, so Henry fired again. Cleveland toppled backward, staring straight up for all time.

Buck Stinson, who had a barber chair in the back of the saloon, had stopped cutting a man's hair when the fight started. Soon as it was over, Buck turned back to his customer and said, "Good riddance!"

The trial was held out on a patch of land between Main Street and Grasshopper Creek on a gray, windy, cold Saturday afternoon, all in accordance with the miners code of justice. Some five hundred folks attended the trial. Benches were brought out of the saloons and placed on the frozen ground, a wagon was drawn up in front of the crowd for Judge Ray Hoyt to sit in. A jury of twelve men were nominated and picked by the crowd who shouted yes or no to each one. Most folks there were bearded miners in dark wool coats and hats.

First witnesses testified how Jack Cleveland had threatened to kill Henry. Then others testified Cleveland had started the fight in the Goodrich, and still others testified that Cleveland was a mean, murdering, low-down bully. Witnesses for Henry were then heard.

They testified he was an honest, hardworking man, brave enough to stand up against the bully Cleveland. Everybody cheered.

The jury of twelve men retired to the Goodrich saloon, and after filling their glasses with whiskey voted twelve to zero for acquittal. When Judge Hoyt pronounced the verdict, the crowd cheered and clapped.

Wasn't long after that a delegation of miners came to Henry and asked if he'd run in the coming election for sheriff—the most powerful job in town, they called it. The town needed a strong sheriff like Henry because the sheriff they had was scared of his own shadow. They had talked to folks in town and found Henry'd acquired a reputation for never saying anything he didn't mean, never turning away from helping somebody in trouble, and never refusing a drink of whiskey.

So Henry ran in the May election against a man named Durley who spoke for the merchants and trades-people in town, the respectable folk. They wanted a sheriff who would be better for business and immigration. Henry won by a large margin, 307 to 247.

Chapter Twenty-Five

COUPLE WEEKS AFTER THAT MEETING in the sheriff's office, I got an invitation for Sunday breakfast at the Sanders place. Wouldn't you know, it was a Sunday morning, and I had a hellfire hangover. On my way there, I had to stop on the bridge over Grasshopper Creek and throw up in the water.

The Sanders cabin was in Yankee Flat where the Union folks lived, the Confederates inclining to the other side of town. Henry Plummer's cabin was just off Main Street, sort of in between the two camps.

I was greeted by the colonel and his wife Hattie, their two small boys jumping up and down like Mexican beans, a servant girl they'd brought with them, and a boy named Henry Tilden. All six of them were smiling away with that twelve-gauge cheerfulness that makes a fella with a hangover even sicker.

Although the Sanders cabin was only one large room, the colonel's wife Hattie had spruced it up nice and cozy. A neat stack of lodgepole pine was burning in the fireplace—it was cold up there in October—and a fancy clock sat on the mantel. She had hung white sheets on the rough log walls for decoration. I noticed he had a case of books which included a large family Bible, a book of speeches by Henry Clay, Dr. Gunn's family medicine, a book called *Paradise Lost* by John Milton, and the book my pa read us at the table, *Uncle Tom's Cabin*.

BANNACK

At first I was interested in Henry Tilden cause he was fifteen years old and I thought maybe could be a friend. Turned out he was Colonel Sanders's nephew and was eager to say *yes-yes-yes* to everything the colonel said. I can't stomach an ass-licker. The servant girl, whose name I never got, looked to be in her twenties. I thought she might be good for a dance or a kiss, but when she started talking, it reminded me what mama once said about God not handing out brain evenly. She giggled at everything, funny or not. But she also had a waist that curved in like an hourglass and a pair of tits my eyes wouldn't take leave of, the kind that stick in a man's memory long afterward.

After we sat down to breakfast, I noticed that Hattie Sanders called her husband Mister. "Mister Sanders," she said, as if she was addressing God himself, "would you like some more coffee?" If that wasn't the damnedest thing. I couldn't imagine my mama calling Pa Mister Mayfair. More likely she'd say, *Mister Hypocrite, would you like some more coffee?* The breakfast was good, though. Mrs. Sanders served a big pot full of hot cereal and a heaping plate of homemade rolls that spread a sweet cinnamon smell through the whole cabin. I devoured rolls like a hungry savage, even though I still had those shooting pains in my belly.

I was a little uneasy at first about what to say, but that turned out to be a waste of worry. All I had to do was ask the colonel a question about himself, and he was off like Fast Jim Hatch.

He said he'd grown up in the western part of New York State. His father was a dedicated Methodist and a stickler for hard work and saving money. His mother was a strong-minded abolitionist who had a sharp eye for spotting evil wherever it might show its nasty face. Freedom Edgerton Sanders was her name, and she smoked a corncob pipe.

By the time he was eight, the colonel said, his mother Freedom had him standing on the kitchen table reciting passages from the Bible. She'd point the stem of her pipe at him and brag to the neighbors he was the smartest boy around.

In school, Colonel Sanders said, he became famous for reciting long passages from the Old Testament on stage in front of other students. He said his teachers told him the same thing as my mother, that he was the smartest boy around, and he came to recognize it was true. Didn't make him popular, telling people that, but he thought saying the truth was more important than being popular.

The colonel said he taught school for a while but had a hankering to do more. So, at the encouragement of his mother, he studied law under the watchful eye of her brother, Sidney Edgerton. At the time Edgerton was a Republican Congressman from Ohio. After several years of hard work getting a certificate, Sanders started his own law practice. He also spent a year in the army, got hitched to Hattie, and had two boys.

The fellas at the Elkhorn told me later that Sanders was a liar about his time in the military because he'd been a lieutenant in the army, not a colonel, and he'd skedaddled soon as the fighting started. But Sanders defended himself by saying he let folks call him colonel because they liked talking to a man of rank. He did it for their sake.

Anyway, Sanders said that while he was in Ohio practicing law, he got to know and respect Sidney Edgerton. In June of 1863 the Sanders and Edgerton families left Omaha in an ox-drawn wagon along with a dozen or so other families headed west. Took three months and two days to reach Bannack, covering over 1,600 miles in something better than fifteen miles a day. At night they sat around the campfire reading from the Bible, singing, songs and telling stories. A few times Colonel Sanders stood up before everyone and told them they were driven by the word of God to replenish the earth and to have dominion over every living thing that moveth upon it. Amen. He loved to preach.

Course Colonel Sanders wasn't the only person to talk at the breakfast table. Hattie liked to talk about the Indians who had a camp not far from town. "I declare," she proclaimed while serving the hot oatmeal, "these Indians are disgusting creatures. So dirty they give me a shudder. Sometimes," she said, "they peer in my window, and other times they tap on the door begging for food. They don't have a speck of self-reliance."

When breakfast was about over, the colonel announced loudly, "Time for church, Billy." I must have winced or rolled my eyes like Mama used to do when Pa said time for church, because Colonel Sanders added, "Do you good, son, do you good! And don't you worry about being bored because we have Brother Sam preaching today. Brother Sam is a travelling Methodist with the biggest parish in the country, bestowed on him by an agreement in Washington between the Protestant Council and the federal government. He's famous, Billy."

Chapter Twenty-Six

Walking up Main Street, I took notice of two drunk miners on the boardwalk in front of the Elkhorn, passed out against the wall. From across the street where we walked, I heard laughter and yelling inside. Made me chuckle to think what some of the boys inside would say if they saw me walking to church with the Sanders family. It didn't bother me, though, having a foot in each camp. There were things I liked about both.

The church was a log building at the end of the street, and Brother Sam met us at the door wearing his black frock coat buttoned up tight, a white shirt, and a high-crowned hat. He was thin as President Lincoln and had eyes that looked eager to grab anybody that came his way.

When everyone was seated on the wood benches inside, Brother Sam strode to the pulpit in front and raised his arms in a big V and said, "Brothers and sisters, I bring you glad tidings! Our own Colonel Chivington, the man who gave up his personal life as a Methodist minister to take up arms against the Indian savages, has won a major victory at the battle of Sand Creek." Brother Sam peered over steel-rimmed glasses riding low on his nose while the folks in the congregation said amen. Then he continued.

"It took place down in Colorado, my friends. Chivington and his troopers charged into the Indian camp at sunrise with guns blazing and bayonets slashing and killed nearly every man, woman, and child there, some five hundred redskins in all. No pussyfooting around this time, a real housecleaning!" He smiled. "If that doesn't send those savages a lesson, I don't know what will."

He stopped a minute and cleared his throat. "Of course, there's a lot of sickly sentimentalists back east sitting in the safety and comfort of their homes wailing and bawling, but those eastern lilies don't understand that when a man is doing God's work, he has no choice. I am pleased to say Colonel Chivington answered those folks in just three words. 'Nits make lice.'" He paused. "That's right, nits make lice."

I didn't know what Brother Sam meant when he said nits make lice, but it was mighty clear the Indians took an awful beating at Sand Creek, and the white folks here were real glad about it. Since I was one of the white folks, I reckoned I ought to be glad about it too.

Brother Sam smiled and gazed around at the folks staring back, then called for everyone to join him in "The Battle Hymn of the Republic." I didn't sing, but I took notice how Colonel Sanders sang so loud his wife Hattie looked at him red-faced with embarrassment. "Glory, glory, hallelujah," he sang, "glory, glory, hallelujah."

The singing voices boomed through the church so loud I thought they might raise the roof. 'Course, they didn't, but they raised my spirits so high, I finally joined in with everybody else. "He's stamping out the vintage with his terrible swift sword…"

Brother Sam went on talking, but my mind started to wander. I hadn't seen Boone or Jack since the flag burning, they got me so damn mad. But I also kind of missed their evil company. It seemed like I had a hankering for the low life as strong as my hankering for making a fortune in gold. I remembered Pa once saying, "Billy, the purpose for being on earth is to fight the battle between good and evil, with hell to pay if you lose." Seemed like good and evil was nearly in the balance in me.

Then Brother Sam said something that caught my attention. He said he'd been contemplating the word of God in Genesis, and he'd reached the conclusion that although all the races of mankind were created on the same day—the seventh and last day of creation—not all the races were created at the same instant. "I am driven to believe that God created the white man first," he said, "probably early morning, and after a few hours or so he created the yellow man, and after that he created the black man, and finally, getting toward sunset, he created the red man." Brother Sam looked around real satisfied with himself. "In other words, my friends, God created mankind in separate stages. The Indians were created last, and that's why they lag behind; that's why they are the most primitive and savage of all the races."

Well, I had to think about that. It made a certain sense, I supposed, but I had to wonder.

After the sermon was over, everyone stepped outside into the cool October air. The men wore their usual black frock coats and chattered away like blackbirds. The women had on their best Sunday dresses and those funny bonnets shaped like shovels, wool shawls around their shoulders for warmth.

I stood next to Colonel Sanders and listened to the conversation between him and the other men, including that fella with such a mean reputation called X Beidler. X was in good spirits and declared loudly how much he favored the sermon that day.

Sanders cleared his throat and said, "From my study of human nature, gentlemen, I have come to believe that when you arrive at a dangerous place like Bannack, you must quickly identify who your friends are and who your enemies are. Once that's done you have to act without mercy toward your enemies. Otherwise they'll come back to hurt you."

"Hear! Hear!" X Beidler said.

As the conversation went on another man muttered, "I wonder if the Italians and Irish were created the exact same time as the rest of us."

Jim Williams replied, "Just because they're lazy and unreliable don't mean they aren't part of the same human race."

"I saw an Eye-talian the other day on the street," another man said. They all shook their heads at this news.

Someone added, "A bunch o' Chinese are nesting down in Virginia City, and there ain't nothin you can do about it."

X Beidler said, "I see the Jews are comin too, haulin in merchandise from Salt Lake City."

By this time I was getting pretty confused by the whole bunch of them, so I slipped out and bolted down the street to the Elkhorn. Might as well go to hell, I thought, if those fellas were going to heaven.

Chapter Twenty-Seven

BY THE TIME NOVEMBER CAME along, I found myself drifting back into the company of Boone and Jack. They'd promised Henry to shut up about the war, so at least once a week we got together at the Elkhorn and drank and told stories and threw insults at each other. I was getting better at that, too. For instance, one night I said, "You cornhole any prairie dogs lately, Boone? That bein about the right fit for ya."

He looked at me with eyebrows raised like he'd just seen a cow dance on two legs. Then said, "Looky here, Jack, this little bugger's getting hisself a tongue. Only trouble is, he's got a brain about the size of a rat's asshole."

Jack shook his head. "That's better'n you. You got shit for brains."

Boone laughed out loud.

But even Valley Tan couldn't chase away the boredom of those long nights in the saloon listening to the same stories with the same fellas. Especially the same fellas, no women around to spice things up.

During those long nights I saw a good bit of Henry Plummer, too. He made a habit of coming down to the Goodrich to visit because he was on his own now. Electa had promised to visit her folks that year and had gone back east to Ohio. Before leaving she had tried to talk Henry into going too, saying Ohio was a better place to live and raise a family, but he braced at that idea. Henry liked his job as sheriff and had even applied for the position of US Marshall in the territory, which he was promised he'd get. Still, he missed Electa and said he couldn't wait for her to get back.

Another thing I learned while talking there in the Goodrich was something about the sheriff's troubles back in California. Francis Thompson, the merchant who owned the dry goods store, told me about this, commencing with how the sheriff had grown up in the state of Maine and had come out to California in 1850 with the big immigration from the east. From San Francisco he sailed up the Sacramento River to Sacramento and then overland to Nevada City, where the miners had struck a mother lode.

Instead of being a miner, though, he first ran a store in town and then ran for the job of marshall, which he won at the age of twenty-five. He became the youngest marshall ever elected in California. He was so popular with the folks in town that he got reelected, which usually didn't happen because the marshall had so many unpopular things to do. But he got himself reelected because he was smart and fearless and because everybody thought he treated folks fairly. He tracked down some of the worst outlaws in the state, boys like Timbuctoo Webster, Big John Sullivan, Rattlesnake Dick, and Shorty Gehr, mean as snakes, all of them, and he brought them in.

His trouble started with a woman who came to him because her husband had been beating her senseless. Henry recommended she leave the sonofabitch because he'd just continue doing the same thing. But when her husband, John Vedder, heard what Henry said, he swore to kill him.

Then one night when Henry was sitting in his house talking with Lucy Vedder, the husband came in the back door drunk and shouted, "Yer time's up, Marshall," and proceeded to fire the first shot. But Henry put three loads into him before he knew what was happening. Then, when Vedder turned to run, Henry fired two more into his back for good measure. That was one thing the jury didn't like, the way Henry kept firing after Vedder was helpless. That wasn't the main thing, though. The jury also didn't like Henry interfering in another man's marriage, wasn't his business, and they really got angry to hear the prosecutor say Henry was having a sexual liaison with Lucy Vedder.

Nobody knows whether that story was true or not, but the jury believed it and found him guilty. The judge sentenced Henry to San Quentin. He wasn't there long, only six months, because so many citizens in Nevada City signed petitions saying he was innocent that the governor commuted his sentence.

Francis Thompson also told about another man Henry killed in California. His name was Riley. He was a seccessionist who got drunk and crazy mad one night in a saloon and attacked Henry because he was a damn Unionist. Riley put a twelve-inch scar across his forehead before Henry drew and killed him.

It all reminded me of what Wilbur Sanders had said about the sheriff's "violent" past. It made me think a little differently about Henry, but it didn't change my view of him. I reckoned he fought in self-defense.

What was most interesting to me was all the talk among Henry and the other fellas about politics and war. The two biggest battles that year, at Vicksburg and Gettysburg, showed the tide of war had turned and was now running in favor of the Union. The men at the Goodrich supported the Union and were joyous to hear about Grant raising the flag over the courthouse in Vicksburg. That meant the whole Mississippi Valley was now in Union hands, and the West was as good as won. But the East was a different kettle of fish. The Union had won a victory at Gettysburg in July, which had shown that the rebels couldn't get away with invading the north, but it didn't prove the war was over by a long shot. All the fellas in the Goodrich agreed there was a lot of war still left to fight, a lot more blood still to be shed.

That's what bothered Henry the most was so many boys getting killed. He said according to a newspaper he saw there were over fifty thousand casualties at Gettysburg alone. "You add up the numbers from there and other battles, and I figure over a hundred and fifty thousand boys died in this last year alone. And the year ain't even over." He shook his head. "From where I sit, the best thing to do is to stop the war now and make peace with the damn rebels."

That didn't make sense to me, nor did it to most of the other fellas in the Goodrich. I told him about those awful slave pens I'd seen in St. Louis and asked how anybody could make peace with those hotheads in the South who claimed slavery was even good for the Negroes they had in bondage. There was no talking with folks who thought like that.

Henry said he hated slavery as much as I did but didn't think war was the best way to end it. "Slavery is gonna die anyway, Billy," he told me one night, "war or no war. It's over in England, and Russia just freed the serfs; the French outlawed slavery a long time ago. I say why not buy the slaves from those big plantation owners with money from the federal treasury? It'd be cheaper to buy slaves at eight hundred dollars apiece than continue this damn war. Then those freed slaves could pay back the government some time later."

Henry was what folks called a peace Democrat, or what Colonel Sanders called a damn copperhead. "The whole bunch of them are traitors," the colonel claimed. Still, I knew Henry was no traitor. He told me himself that he had been a member of the Democratic Party back in California, working to elect Stephen Douglas over Abraham Lincoln in 1860, because he thought Lincoln meant war, but that didn't make him a traitor. He had also run for the California legislature and lost because there had been a big fight inside the Democratic Party. If he'd won that election, he would have been the youngest member of the legislature. Still, those things didn't make him a traitor.

The way Henry put it was like this: "That fella Horace Greeley got it right when he said we ought to let those damn seccessionists go: we'd be a better country without 'em. I believe those fools down south would eventually come back on hands and knees to the Union anyway."

I couldn't say I agreed with Henry on that and said so. "I reckon somebody has to be right, and somebody has to be wrong, or this whole damn war don't make sense, Henry."

He shook his head, "The whole damn war don't make sense."

I shook my head. "I can't help it, I hate slavery and believe the Union is right."

But our conversation reminded me of what Mr. Plunkett had said about those young soldiers dying from the ambush, that it didn't make any difference to them who was right or wrong. And it made me think about my own experience working in the army hospital in St. Louis. I mentioned this to the fellas there at the Goodrich, that I had worked for two weeks in a Union hospital, but I was skittish talking about it, so I didn't say much.

Chapter Twenty-Eight

IT WAS CURIOUS HOW WILBUR Sanders latched onto a Masonic funeral to commence his drive to organize a vigilance committee. I guess he saw all those Masons together and reckoned it was time to start.

What happened was this: A merchant by the name of Bell had fallen in the creek on his way home from the saloon one night, but he managed to get up and stagger back to his cabin and pass out on his bed soaking wet. In the morning he was frozen solid as a stick. Ding-Dong Bell, folks called him, would never toll again.

Henry wasn't too surprised. He said death by freezing was the leading cause of dying in Bannack, all those miners passing out in the cold while they were drunk.

Anyway, it turned out Ding-Dong Bell left a letter behind saying he had been a Mason all his life and wanted a Masonic burial. Colonel Sanders, being a Mason himself, took charge.

On the day of the funeral, a heavy snow was falling on Bannack, and the sun was nearly whited out, just a dim round glow in a skyful of whirling flakes. I stood next to Wilbur Sanders's nephew, Henry Tilden, who I tried to avoid most of the time because he was such an ass-licker, but this day we stood together and watched while six stalwart Masons heaved Bell's coffin to their shoulders and started off toward the cemetery at the top of the hill north of town. Thirty or forty men in black overcoats and black hats followed along behind the casket, trudging across the flat and up the steep hill, making a long black train against the white snow, the train rising slowly into the darkness at the top.

I never learned what Colonel Sanders said at the cemetery on top, but it wasn't long till the whole bunch came back down stomping and slipping in silence, wearing grim, determined looks on their faces. They headed directly to Colonel Sanders' cabin as if he'd given them an order. I looked at Henry Tilden, and he looked back at me, and we decided without saying a word we'd find out what was going on.

So we slipped through the door of the Sanders cabin along with a bunch of men and made our way to the back of the room where we could mix unnoticed in the crowd. Everyone stood facing the colonel, who climbed atop a small box near the fireplace and raised his hands to get everybody quieted down.

"Gentlemen," he said, "we are all Masons. This is a meeting of Masons, and according to the rules of our order everyone in this room is sworn to secrecy about what takes place here today. Anyone can't hold to that better get out now."

The colonel looked over the silent crowd, strong men with jaws set and eyes hard on him, then took a deep breath and started firing away. It was a long speech, and I'm not going to bore you with all of it, but I'll give you the main part as close to his words as I can.

He started by saying, "We, all of us decent folks here today, whether we like it or not, are engaged in a deadly war. Yessir, I said war. And I say we'd better stop right now and start thinking about it, because if we don't, God help us, we are in danger of losing everything we hold dear."

He looked around. "As many of you know, renegades and rebels in this town are calling for the defeat of the Union and victory for the Confederacy. They drink to the health of Jefferson Davis, and they burn the American Flag right out in the open to show where their loyalties lie. They conspire and they collude to overthrow the legitimate government of the United States. The rebels are supported by the sweet-talking copperheads who profess to stand for peace but really stand for surrender. They are a disgrace to our boys dying on the battlefields, boys who fight to preserve our freedom and the Union."

Someone from the crowd shouted, "Give 'em hell, Wilbur," and everyone laughed. Colonel Sanders smiled. He was a fierce speaker, all right; his voice was powerful, his eyes firing bolts of lightning.

The colonel went on to say that there was another threat just as bad as the first—the threat of outlaws. "Outlaws have robbed the Peabody stage and waylaid the Magruder wagon train. They have murdered Magruder himself. And that is not all. There are probably a hundred other crimes committed on the trails and back roads of the territory without anyone even knowing about them. Good men leave our community laden with the gold dust of their labor and are never heard from again. We can only conclude they have been robbed and murdered."

"Hear, hear," someone shouted. "You tell 'em, Wilbur." Seemed like the whole room shook from men stomping their feet and clapping their hands.

Well, it was getting mighty hot in this little cabin by now, all those stalwart men in heavy coats pressed together and the colonel firing words like bullets.

"Who are these traitors and outlaws?" Colonel Sanders called out loudly. "Ask yourself that, gentlemen. We are not a big community. No other communities exist nearby. Who are the traitors and outlaws? Are they the decent and honorable people we see and do business with every day?" He waited a second while everyone shook their heads. "Well, if it's not us," he declared, "it must be somebody else." He looked around again, his forehead dripping sweat, his eyes gleaming. "I don't have to tell you their names because you know them. You know who they are. They are the vermin who inhabit the saloons of this town. They don't believe in the Union. They don't believe in honest work. They are godless degenerates who don't go to church and are protected from the law by the law itself. Yes, you heard me, protected by the law itself!"

He paused to let his words sink in. "These degenerates are men who have no control over themselves. They not only drink to drunkenness, they even do vile things with other men in violation of the most sacred law handed down by God."

The crowd was now dead quiet. I don't know what he said that made everyone quiet down, but I could hear my heart thump. Everyone stood in silence with their mouths open.

"My friends," he said, softly now, "we are a good folk living in a good land. No nation on the face of the earth or in recorded history has had such a godly origin. We have inherited from our ancestors a covenant with God to establish dominion over this vast country, to subdue our enemies and multiply our race. We have a manifest destiny that will light the way for all nations. Mark my words. One day the whole world will speak the Anglo-Saxon tongue and practice the same religion and have the same laws as the Anglo-Saxon race."

The colonel paused and let a moment of silence settle like fine dust over the crowd.

All of a sudden I felt scared. It wasn't just his words, it was a feeling of being surrounded by men who were different from me and might see me as part of the enemy Sanders was talking about. I wasn't supposed to be there, and I'd heard things I wasn't supposed to hear. I glanced over at Henry Tilden and saw he was looking all excited and proud of his uncle up there delivering his sermon. I eased off to the side and slipped through the crowd to the door and slunk out without anyone even noticing.

It was a relief to breathe the cold dry air. The light snow lay softly over the ground, and light from the cabin windows reached out into the dusky night air. I kicked my way through the snow and over the bridge and down the street, past the lights and noise of the saloons, to the Goodrich. I reckoned I'd better tell the sheriff about this meeting of the Masons.

Chapter Twenty-Nine

NEXT DAY, WHEN I TOLD the sheriff what Colonel Sanders had said, he rubbed his chin and pondered a while and then just shrugged. "I suppose I'd better talk to Wilbur," he muttered, "make sure he don't go off half-cocked."

But he didn't seem to think it was something to worry about. He reckoned this was just the colonel's way of making a name for himself and building up his law practice. "Sounds like he's runnin for political office, don't it?"

By this time of year I was no longer working on Henry's claims; I was off searching and digging on my own. One thing I found out real quick was no use searching east of town where the creek flowed across a flat plain; it was better in the rocky soil of the hills where Mother Nature had tossed the gold up closer to the surface.

Let me tell you, though, in November the weather was mighty cold, Grasshopper Creek frozen around the edges, the ground hard as stone. I bought a secondhand overcoat and a wool hat and gloves but still couldn't chase out the cold. When I came home at night, my hands were red and swollen, aching from being in the cold water.

I didn't dig as much gold, either. In the months of September, October, and November, I averaged only about five dollars a day. I say "only" because back home that would have been a lot, but not here, where the living was expensive and I was expecting to make a fortune. All told I made about three hundred dollars during that time and saved eighty-five of it. Not bad for back home, but not enough for being out here in the wilderness.

That's when I decided to try something called dry panning. What this meant was I had to climb up away from the creek through the gulches and dry washes that creased through the hills, then swing a pick to break up the ground before shoveling the rocks and dirt into the pan. After that I had to shake and bang the pan to get the heavy stuff to filter down and then pick off the rocks and debris with my fingers.

The first few days I came up with next to nothing. I guess it was on the seventh day it happened, when I was about to give up and go back to the creek. That day had started out real cold, the frost on the ground so thick it crackled under my boots, the air so crisp it froze the hairs in my nose. I stood near the top of a steep dry wash that looked like it carried a lot of runoff in the spring and saw a single sagebrush growing up in front of a big, smooth rock, and I remembered what Boone had said once about how gold stuck to the roots of sagebrush. Several times I drove the pick into the rocky soil around the sagebrush and then with my shovel I turned the plant over, roots and all, and spotted a dark, jagged lump of soil that stopped me in my tracks. I wiped it off, and there it was, the color, the gold, the first genuine nugget I ever found. I dropped to my knees and held it in front of me as if I was holding the Holy Grail.

After that I worked like a beaver, picking, smashing, banging as fast and hard as I could. I had struck a small lode of gold right in front of the rock. I picked up about fifteen nuggets of varying sizes that first day, every so often looking around to make sure nobody was watching me. I was determined to work the whole area out by myself before anyone else got to know about it.

That night I went to the Elkhorn and had a swig with the boys, but I didn't say a thing. That was the hardest of all, sitting there with that secret screaming to get out.

Next day I went out and brought back another small load of flakes and nuggets and cached them in my room at the Goodrich. The third day it snowed, and while the other miners stayed put, I tramped out. That was a mistake. Some miners noticed I was out in the blowing snow and wondered why. The following day a couple of them sneaked after me to the site of my little mother lode, and that was the end of my secret. I hadn't staked a claim, so everyone attacked the area like locusts, and it was cleaned out in two days.

I couldn't complain, though. I brought all my nuggets and flakes and dust to Crisman's store, got it weighed, and just about shit my pants to learn I had over sixteen hundred dollars. I cached seven hundred of it in Henry's safe and the nine hundred in the safe at the Goodrich. I was rich.

Seemed like the quality folks were more friendly to me after that, smiled more often as I walked by. "Hello there, Billy, how are you today?" Hattie Sanders stopped me on the street and asked when I was coming back for dinner.

The daughter of Judge Sidney Edgerton, Mattie Edgerton, a fourteen-year-old spoiled brat who'd never bothered before to glance at me, said "Hello, Billy, you going to the Thanksgiving Day dinner?"

Chapter Thirty

THE SHERIFF GAVE A BIG Thanksgiving dinner in order to smooth things out between himself and the churchgoing folks in town, thinking mainly of Wilbur Sanders and Sidney Edgerton. He wanted them on his side instead of opposing him or even doing something real foolish like organizing a vigilance committee, which Wilbur Sanders had been blabbing about. Henry had seen other vigilantes hang two innocent men in California and was dead set against them; he swore they'd set foot in Bannack over his dead body.

The dinner was prepared by Martha Vail. The Vails, James and Martha, had managed the government farm at Sun River where Henry met Electa. To nobody's surprise, the farm had failed because the Indians scorned being farmers. So at Henry's invitation, the Vails had moved to Bannack, and James went to work on one of Henry's claims. Martha Vail, Electa's sister, who was first opposed to Electa marrying Henry, changed her opinion of Henry completely and became so friendly toward him, some people began gossiping about it, especially since Electa had gone back east. Henry Tilden, my ass-kisser friend, said he'd overheard his uncle Colonel Sanders say he thought the sheriff was a scoundrel by leading Martha on.

Anyway, the dinner was prepared by Martha Vail, and it turned out to be the biggest and richest dinner ever put on in Bannack. Henry ordered a whole cartload of food from Salt Lake City, including a forty-pound turkey that by itself cost forty dollars. Everyone thought he must have a lot of money from his mining claims cached away in that safe of his in Crisman's store. Martha Vail stuffed the turkey with a lot of store-bought spices, and it came out of the oven smelling as good as my mama's Thanksgiving Day turkey, which was the best I ever tasted. Besides the turkey, there was canned oysters, fruit salad made of little pieces of chopped up fruit with whipped cream and a cherry on top, mashed potatoes and gravy, sweet potatoes, three different vegetables, two different kinds of cheese I'd never heard of before, mince pie, and sweet chocolates imported from Switzerland. But what made everybody ooh and ahh was four different kinds of wine from France, which was served in special glasses next to every plate. Every single person there was in a state of shock at the richness of it all.

I'd never tasted wine before, and when I did, I wondered why anyone even liked it. It didn't have the whack of whiskey or the sweetness of cider: it was like drinking dust. At the end of the dinner, though, someone poured me a tiny glass of what they called brandy, and that was a bolt of lightning just like whiskey.

At the beginning of dinner Wilbur Sanders stood up and raised his glass in honor of Henry. "Our thanks to you, Sheriff," he said, "and good wishes for a long and healthy life."

Henry seemed pleased by this. That's when he told me his main purpose in having the dinner was to promote peace in Bannack and to let Edgerton know that he was not against his and Wilbur's plan to make a new territory out of the territory east of the Bitter Root mountains, which is to say eastern Idaho.

Must have been three dozen people there at the dinner, mostly merchants and professional people, but there were a few miners too, including a man named Bill Fairweather who had made a big discovery over at Virginia City in Alder Gulch. In one strike he'd become as rich as the King of England, folks said. Because of Fairweather's discovery, the town of Virginia City was growing bigger than Bannack. Like most of the miners, though, old Bill Fairweather eventually lost his fortune through drinking and gambling. At the dinner party, no one was surprised to see him so drunk his eyes looked crossed.

Because I had struck it rich too, I walked around with a brand-new sense of self respect. I had bought myself a suit a clothes at Crisman's for the occasion, including a white shirt and tie and bowler hat, something I'd never worn before in my life, and besides that I got a haircut and shave at the Goodrich from Buck Stinson, although Buck said the only thing he found to shave off was a little fuzz. Anyway, I was dolled up like a steamboat gambler.

Mattie Edgerton, the spoiled brat who'd asked if I was going to the dinner, came over and asked me in her uppity way if I was also going to the dance next Saturday night. She allowed as she was, and she'd even do me the favor of dancing with her if I wanted to. She also added that she wouldn't mind dancing with the sheriff either, he was so handsome, except he was a Democrat, and she didn't dance with Democrats because they were traitors. I told her she was full of baloney. I should have said "shit" instead of "baloney," but didn't.

Her mother, Mary Edgerton, sat at the table like a queen, and after the dinner I walked over to hear what she was saying to her husband, Judge Edgerton. "This is the most sumptuous dinner I've seen since we were in Washington, Sidney." I was standing off to one side pretending to be interested in something else. "Henry Plummer is so charming and gracious, it makes me wonder why you talk so badly about him."

Hearing that, I wondered what Judge Edgerton and Wilbur Sanders were saying that was so bad about Henry. Later that evening I saw a chance. They were standing with their heads together, not noticing anyone else around them. I couldn't hear much, but I caught the word "Scandalous." Someone was doing something scandalous. They were standing at a table with the brandy and wine on it, which Wilbur Sanders didn't drink because he was Temperance. I moseyed over and poured myself a little bit of the brandy. Sanders saw me and said, "You're too young to be drinking that, son."

I put it down, feeling stupid, and walked over to the wall just behind them where they were standing. That's when I heard Judge Edgerton say, "If we're going to succeed in Washington, Wilbur, we have to do it …" He stopped and turned around to see if anyone could hear and saw me. I had to scoot without catching anything more. I didn't know what to make of it anyway.

I cast a glance at Martha during the dinner and had to admit the colonel was right about one thing: she stared at Henry with eyes I'd seen once in a sick calf. She liked him, all right. But I didn't think she was betraying her husband or Henry was betraying Electa. That's something I never would know for sure.

Anyway, I was feeling real good about myself. All that money I had cached away gave me the feeling I was the luckiest fella ever lived. It made me think I was probably going home next spring not with a fortune but a rich man, enough anyway to gain the respect of Pa. This was the most joyous Thanksgiving I ever had.

Chapter Thirty-One

By December Bannack was under siege of winter. The dark gray clouds thundered in from the north like huge boulders rolling across the sky, and the bitter cold got a hard grip on everything and everybody. First week of December a blizzard struck so hard it left snow piled up in six-foot drifts against the Elkhorn. On Main Street the ground was blowed bare in some spots and humped up in ridges in others where the snow caught on something and stuck. I took notice one day of a pile of fresh horseshit giving off steam like water on hot coals.

Everybody with any sense holed up.

It was a time for all-day drinking in the Elkhorn, the miners packed in wall to wall, slurping from morning to night. One night I was in the Elkhorn and watched Haze Lyons drink to where he couldn't move any longer, couldn't even talk, just sat there in his chair, leaning this way and that, till finally he toppled forward like a chopped tree. A wonder he didn't break his nose. Some boys were half asleep sitting in their chairs, and others were passed out in the bunks along the back wall. I saw some miners staggering out that night into the icy air and wondered if they were about to enter into eternity.

Made me wonder what God said when a man showed up at the pearly gates dead drunk. Told him to come back after he sobered up, I suppose.

BANNACK

Although it was a boring time, and most boys were feeling irritable, I have to say I felt good. I was rich and so full of high spirits that I bought a cabin. It wasn't much to look at, about ten by twelve feet in size and made of rough logs, only one room, not a stick of furniture and no windows, but it cost me just three hundred dollars. It was chinked solid against the weather and had a good fireplace that kept the room warm and cozy while it was below zero outside.

It also gave me something to do. I made a solid bed of wood planks, a table, and straight chairs and hauled in a big supply of firewood. I also shot several deer and an elk for their hides as well as meat and made a spread for the bed and the dirt floor. Henry taught me how to cure the skins for the blanket and rug; the extra meat I gave to the Goodrich in exchange for free meals.

Anyway, these doings kept me from slurping Valley Tan all day at the Elkhorn. The two or three nights I went in to drink with Boone and Jack, I took it slow and easy and sat there thinking the whole saloon was half dead. Sometimes half an hour'd go by, and nobody had said a word. Some nights it was like a tomb, other nights a circus.

Then near the end of December something happened that woke everybody up. A young man named Nick Tiebolt was robbed and murdered over near Virginia City. Henry had a deputy over there, Buz Caven, and Buz sent back the news through one of those lowlife spies Henry had working for him named Clubfoot George Lane.

I was with Henry in his office when Clubfoot George brought in the news. He said the young fella murdered, Nick Tiebolt, was only seventeen years old and liked by everybody because he lit up any room he walked into. So when his body was brought into town and put on public display, his eyes picked out by crows and his neck all burned from being dragged, the folks got up in arms. Real arms. A posse was rounded up on the spot, and half a dozen men rode out without even telling Buz Caven what they were up to. The posse tracked down a man called Long John Frank who was living with George Ives, near the scene of the crime, and the posse scared Long

John into confessing his friend George Ives was the murderer. So George Ives and Long John Frank had been arrested and were now sitting in jail in Virginia City.

But that wasn't all, Clubfoot George said. Wilbur Sanders and a couple others got folks so riled up by their speeches, everybody demanded a trial right away. So the trial of George Ives was starting that very day. Buz Caven tried to slow things down till the sheriff got there, but he was overruled by the others. The trial was being held just south of Virginia City, and Wilbur Sanders was the prosecutor, James Thurmond the defense lawyer for Ives, and Judge Warren Byam was presiding. Buz Caven had joined with Judge Byam in picking a jury of twenty-four men, but he had nothing to do but watch after that.

Clubfoot George ended by saying he thought Wilbur Sanders was getting too big for his britches, taking the law in his own hands, and that the sheriff ought to go over and get things under his control. But Henry didn't want to. He said there wasn't anything he could do once the trial got started, and it had already started. He also said he trusted Buz to keep him informed of what was happening.

Then he turned to me and said, "What about you, Billy? You want to go over and keep track of what's goin on?"

So I left on the noon stage to Virginia City.

Chapter Thirty-Two

AFTER SPENDING A NIGHT AT one of the way-stations, I got into Virginia City the next day.

As usual it was cold, probably twenty degrees below zero—Jack would say colder than a whore on her day off—and ten inches of snow lay on the ground. But the sun blazed away in a clear blue sky, and that bright sunshine in the dry mountain air made it feel warmer than the thermometer said.

The trial was going full speed ahead when I got to the little village just south of Virginia City. In the center of the village where the snow was all packed down two wagons had been drawn together to form the front of the courtroom. Benches had been laid out for the twenty-four members of the jury, tables set over to one side for the prosecutor and defense. Back of this a big crowd of spectators stood on the snow-packed road, stamping their feet and pressing in close together to keep warm. Must have been fifteen hundred people all told. A huge bonfire blazed away on one side of the road.

I squeezed through the crowd to a spot near the fire to watch the proceedings. Judge Byam sat in one of the two wagons in front with his hat and coat and gloves on; the defendants Long John Frank and George Ives sat in the other wagon. George Ives was smiling and waving to friends in the crowd like he wasn't the least bit scared. He was a handsome young fella, only a couple years older than me, with a slab of yellow hair down one side of his face, clean-shaven but still wearing an old dirty coat. Long John Frank sat beside him staring at nothing in particular. I reckoned Colonel Sanders had cleaned Long John up for the trial, haircut and shave, clean clothes. The fella next to me said he never saw Long John so spick-and-span in his life, hardly recognized the old bugger.

Colonel Sanders was on his feet at the center of things, dressed in a fine black overcoat on top of his usual frock coat, pacing back and forth on the packed snow and telling what a no-good heathen scoundrel George Ives was. The colonel called witnesses to the stand who told how Ives got drunk and picked fights, borrowed money and never paid it back, and in general made life miserable for decent, honest folks. Then the colonel used a word I'd never heard before; he said George Ives was a villainous libertine.

But the defense lawyer, James Thurmond, who also had on his overcoat and looked like he'd maybe taken a swig too many to warm up, had another say about that. He called George Ives a young man who sometimes got wild when he was drinking but was really a decent boy at heart and certainly not a thief or killer. "There's not a scintilla of evidence to support that claim," Thurmond said, "not a shred of evidence." He brought witnesses forward to testify Ives was a gentleman with the ladies and that he was kind to animals and loved his mother as much as the next man. When Ives was sober, he was a picture of rectitude, Thurmond said; only when he was drunk was he sometimes a little troublesome.

Thurmond was no match for Sanders, though, when it came to sounding off. Thurmond spoke like a kindly old uncle, while Sanders put the fear of hell in his voice.

The afternoon went on like this for a long time, both sides trading potshots at each other, till late in the day when things came to a head. That's when Colonel Sanders called Long John Frank to the witness stand.

As I said, Long John looked all slicked up for the occasion. When the colonel asked him questions, he answered "yessir" or "nossir" just like that ass-kissing pot-licker Henry Tilden. Then the Colonel told Long John to tell why the murdered young man, Nick

Tiebolt, also called the Dutchman, had come to their place that fatal day. Long John said the Dutchman was there to fetch mules from Ives, who took care of them on his small ranch. When Tiebolt paid George Ives, he flashed a big wad of bills that made George's eyes light up. After Tiebolt left, George came to him, Long John, and said, "Hell, the Dutchman don't need all that money." Then, according to Long John, Ives lit out after the Dutchman.

"Why didn't you stop him?" Sanders asked.

Long John shook his head, and said, "Because I was scared George might kill me."

Then Sanders asked Long John to describe what happened next.

Long John said, "I waited around the ranch till George got back about noon with a big smile on his face. I asked him what he was smilin about, and he said he done caught up with Tiebolt and told the boy to fork over his money or he'd kill him. Tiebolt forked over his money, and then George just laughed and said, 'Shit, I'm gonna kill you anyway.' The Dutchman started cryin and pleadin for some time to pray before he was shot. George said he told the Dutchman 'All right, just kneel down and I'll give ya some time to pray.'"

Colonel Sanders held up both hands and stopped Long John. "Now listen to me carefully, Long John, I want you to tell us the exact words George Ives said to you."

Long John threw a glance at the jury, then looked back at Sanders. "George Ives said to me, 'When the Dutchman kneeled down and commenced to pray, I shot him in the head.'"

The colonel turned around slowly toward the jury and cried, "When he kneeled down and commenced to pray, I shot him in the head." Then he whirled back around and raised his arm like a rifle aimed at Ives and shouted, "He hurls defiance at heaven itself with his arrogance. That man murdered Nick Tiebolt in cold blood!"

Those words caused quite a stir in the crowd.

The defense lawyer Thurmond seemed shocked at first. Then he rose, a little unsteady on his feet, shuffled over to Long John and said, "I got one question for you Long John. Did you get immunity from prosecution by testifying against Ives?"

Long John said, "Yes sir, I did."

Thurmond turned to the jury and smiled. "You see, gentlemen, Long John testifies against Ives, and he goes free. You can't take the word of a known liar and use those words to condemn a man."

Then Thurmond sat down. But just as he was sitting down Long John hollered back at him, "Hey there, Mr. Thurmond, I also told that same story before I got immunity."

Thurmond looked like he'd seen Satan himself. He didn't say anything, just stood there dazed. By now it was getting dark, and several men had lit more bonfires and set torches in the ground. Thurmond's face was lit up by the firelight so everyone could see his confusion. The flames also cast dancing shadows across the men and wagons and tables of the makeshift court.

No matter what was said after that, I could see the testimony by Long John outweighed everything else. In fact I reckoned Ives's goose was cooked. So when the jury trooped off and deliberated and a few minutes later straggled back to say the verdict was twenty-three for guilty and one for acquittal, I wasn't surprised.

On hearing this, the colonel leapt to his feet, casting a long shadow in the firelight, and cried, "Justice delayed is justice denied. I move that George Ives be forthwith hanged by the neck till he is dead."

A storm of cries erupted from the crowd, the yeas drowning out the nays.

The colonel glanced over at the man in charge of the prisoners, Jim Williams, and Williams waved for his men to step forward. Must have been two dozen men came out from behind the wagons and stood with rifles at the ready, facing a handful of men who had strode forward with pistols drawn to stop the hanging. The men with pistols were so outnumbered, they couldn't do anything but stand there.

Jim Williams glared at the men with pistols. He was a quiet, respected man in town, but folks said if Williams set out to do something, nothing this side of hell could stop him. He strode over to the wagon, grabbed Ives by the arm, and made him climb down to the ground. His men with rifles made a circle around Ives so I couldn't see him, and then the whole group started marching forward at the command of Colonel Sanders.

The storming crowd of onlookers surged forward after Williams and Sanders, but they were held back by a dozen men who held their rifles like shields to keep the crowd in line. Some folks were shouting to stop this right now, and others were shouting, "Banish him, don't kill him." But Sanders and Williams weren't listening.

I rushed out ahead and saw where the whole bunch was going. It was an unfinished log house with a bonfire burning to one side of it. The light from the fire lit up a beam sticking straight out in front with a rope hanging down from it, a hangman's noose dangling at the end of the rope, and a wood crate underneath. Standing by the crate was a smiling X Beidler, the man who had volunteered and was turned down by Henry to do the Horan hanging. Some folks said X was a righteous man; others said he was the most bloodthirsty rat in the territory. Henry Plummer said he was both.

In the eastern sky a pale moon was rising.

Williams and his men marched Ives over to the unfinished log building while the other men held the crowd back a distance. For a while I couldn't see Ives, surrounded by all those men with rifles, but when Williams brought him out into the open, Ives looked like he didn't know what was going on; his hair was messed, his coat was gone, and he was stumbling around like he was off balance. X grabbed Ives by the arm and jammed the barrel of his pistol under Ive's chin, forcing him to step up on the wood crate. Then X fixed the rope around his neck and tightened the knot behind his right ear.

When X stood back and left George Ives standing there all by himself on the crate, the crowd suddenly fell dead silent, not a whisper anywhere.

Sanders cried out, "George Ives, have you got any last words?" Ives looked scared to death now, his eyes searching around for somebody to help him. It looked like he was trying to say something, but nothing came out of his mouth. Sanders called out again, "Might as well confess!"

Ives cried, "I'm innocent." He saw X stepping forward to kick the crate out from under him and yelled, "Alex Carter killed the Dutchman."

X kicked the crate out from under Ives, and when he hit the end of the rope with a thud, I felt an awful shudder in my own body. Made me grit my teeth seeing him squirm and twist there in the light of the bonfire, but still I couldn't take my eyes away: it was so horrible I had to keep looking.

Afterward I hurried back to my hotel in town and crawled into bed. *Ives was probably guilty*, I kept telling myself, *he got what he deserved*, but I woke up the next morning still telling myself the same thing. I guess no one will ever know for sure.

Chapter Thirty-Three

THE DAY AFTER THE IVES trial Wilbur Sanders strode up the main street of Virginia City with his top hat tipped back, his shoulders straighter than usual, and a big smile on his face. "Damn if he don't look like he has a feather up his ass," one fella said.

Truth is most folks in town were much obliged by what Wilbur had done in the Ives trial. One fella passed him on the street and called out, "You're a hard man, Wilbur."

Sanders shouted back, "It's a hard country."

Colonel Sanders entered the mercantile store owned by Paris Pfouts and strode to the back room where he was joined by Pfouts, Jim Williams, X Beidler and several others who were under Williams command at the Ives trial. No one knows exactly what was said at this meeting because all of them kept their word about secrecy, but everyone in the territory soon found out what happened there because that's where the Vigilance Committee of Virginia City was born.

So here's my version of what happened. I came up with this way of seeing it by figuring backward, going from what they did afterward to what they must have decided to do to begin with.

Sanders took charge. He was the brains behind it all: he was the smartest, shrewdest, toughest, and hardest talker there. He started off by saying they'd just won a big victory in hanging Ives, and now was the time to strike while the iron was hot. Then he explained in his righteous voice how a Vigilance Committee could be organized right there in Virginia City.

"It's not hard, my friends," he said. "First, we have to enlist those men of our community who have a hunger to clean out the vermin. We want the men who do the hard work and don't talk about it later. Then above them comes the Executive Committee. The Executive Committee hears the evidence against any man accused of a crime and on the basis of the evidence makes a recommendation to the president. The president then decides if a man's guilty or not. If guilty, there is only one punishment: death by hanging. The orders are issued by the Executive Committee and are carried out by the men in the field under the leadership of the chief operating officer."

Sanders had a deep voice and a spellbinding manner. The men listening to him didn't say a word, as if they somehow knew this was a historic moment, and they were about to do something that would change their lives and the life of the community. The only sound for a moment was the crack of wood burning in the stove in front of them.

Then Pfouts said, "What you say, Wilbur, makes me think of that Vigilance Committee down in San Francisco. They ran the rats out of town good and proper, strung 'em up for everyone to see."

X added, "No reason we can't do the same thing here."

Before Sanders agreed to draw up the rules governing the conduct of the vigilantes, he said there was one more point needed to be included in the operating rules. That was to include the words: "The assets of the men hanged will be confiscated by the Vigilance Committee and used thereafter to fund future operations and to pay expenses for additional political activities."

"What kind of political activities?" Williams asked.

"What kind? Well, such as a trip to Washington to persuade those politicians back there we need a whole new territory with our government in Bannack. It's the only way we're going to get rid of the damn miners code of law and install a system of justice with our own men in charge."

"What about Sheriff Plummer?" one of the men asked.

Sanders shook his head. "The Vigilance Committee works in place of Plummer, men."

Before the meeting was over, Paris Pfouts was named president, Wilbur Sanders counsel, and Jim Williams chief operating officer. They then proceeded to draw up lists of men to enlist into their ranks, either by an appeal to their principles or by a threat to their lives. Since Williams already had men willing to ride with him, he was given orders to get them together as he had done in capturing George Ives, then set off to find Alec Carter, the man Ives mentioned just before he was hanged.

So the next morning Jim Williams and X Beidler rode out of Virginia City on horseback with eleven other stalwart men who had been sworn in as vigilantes, the army of the Vigilance Committee of Virginia City. Everybody knows what they did after that. Folks might not know why they did it, or the exact details, but they know the facts.

The weather was bitter cold and windy, with new snow already eight inches deep on the wagon road and still falling. The men were dressed for the weather, having stuffed newspaper in their boots and added extra layers of wool underwear, hats pulled down to their ears and scarves tied up to their eyes.

The first place they stopped was Bunton's ranch where they found Red Yeager working as cook and bartender. They knew Yeager was acquainted with Carter, so they asked him at first politely if he knew where Carter was. When Yeager refused to answer, saying it was none of their business, Beidler walked around the bar and stuck the barrel of a pistol under his chin. "Ya got two seconds, Red."

Yeager had second thoughts right away. "Last I heard, he was headin for Cottonwood."

Next day the thirteen vigilantes rode a steady pace through the snow and up through the mountains to the Continental Divide at Deer Lodge Pass, then down through the biting wind and snow into the broad valley where the small settlement of Cottonwood was located. But Alex Carter was nowhere to be found. Instead they found someone who said Carter had been warned the vigilantes were coming, and so he skedadelled. When they asked the man who'd warned Carter, he didn't say at first but also had second thoughts when Beidler drew his pistol. He described somebody who fit the description of Red Yeager, the man who'd told them where to find Carter in the first place.

Williams and Beidler reckoned it must be true. Yeager was the only other person who knew that they were after Carter. So they decided right on the spot to forget about Carter for the time being and go back and have a little talk with Red Yeager. "If Yeager warned Carter, he must know something more," Beidler said.

They found Yeager exactly where they had left him, at the bar at Bunton's ranch. He was half sober and laughing with customers at the bar. Williams and Beidler wasted no time and took him aside to the next room. Beidler said, "Why'd you do it, Red?"

Yeager was silent at first, then said he didn't know what they were talking about. But the pain inflicted by Beidler's pistol gouging into his ear got so worrisome he quickly changed his mind. "Well, I reckoned I had to, boys."

"Why'd you have to?"

Red looked puzzled a moment, then said, "I owed it to Alex for tellin you where he was."

Beidler and Williams looked at each other and laughed. "Well, Red, you just confessed to a hanging offense," Beidler said.

They sat Red down at a table and pulled up two chairs on each side of him. It was cold as ice in the room, and Yeager's hands were shaking badly. Beidler put a bottle of whiskey on the table and told Yeager not to touch it, then said, "Ya committed a hanging offense Red. The only thing can save yer neck is to confess."

Williams nodded. "You know what happened to Long John. He told us Ives killed Tiebolt and got off free."

"Confess to what?" Yeager said. "I tole ya I warned Alex, what else is there?"

Williams stared at him hard. "What else is there? I'll tell what else is there. We've been told by a man in high authority there's a whole gang of outlaws operating in this territory, starting with the men who robbed the Peabody stage, and we want to know who they are. We want their names. Not just some, all of them."

Yeager said, "I never heard of any gang of outlaws."

Beidler quickly muttered, "The only thing's gonna save your ass, Red, is you confess names." He pushed the whiskey bottle over in front of Yeager. "Give us names and take a good swig." Beidler got out pen and paper and laid it on the table in front of him.

"Well, to start with, I don't know all their names," Yeager said.

Beidler cracked Yeager hard on the side of his head with his knuckles. "I got a mind to hang ya right now, Red, no more questions."

Yeager grabbed the bottle of whiskey and threw down a big slug. "Well, there's Alex Carter, like you said, and there's George Brown, George Ives, Long John Frank, George Hilderman." He stopped for another swig of whiskey. "Then there's Boone Helm, Jack Gallagher, Cyrus Skinner, Bill Bunton, Frank Parrish, Haze Lyons, Whiskey Bill Graves, Dutch John Wagner, Johnny Cooper, Joe Pizanthia, Clubfoot George Lane, Buck Stinson."

"Buck Stinson!" Beidler cried. He turned to Williams. "Just like the colonel thought. And just like I thought, too. If Stinson is in this, so is the sheriff." He turned back to Yeager. "What about Henry Plummer, Red, is he the leader of the gang? That's what the colonel thinks, and so do I."

Yeager compressed his lips and nodded his head.

Beidler jumped up, excited. "Get the hell outta here a minute, Red, I gotta talk to Jim."

After Yeager left, Beidler said, "That's all we need, Jim. Only thing left is hang Red Yeager."

Williams looked surprised. "Hang him?"

Beidler was so excited he slammed a fist into his open hand. "You betcher life, hang 'im. You don't think that snake's gonna tell the same story when he gets back to Virginia City, do ya? Hell no, he won't! He'll get hisself a lawyer and get the sheriff on his side and back down from everything." Beidler paced back and forth a minute, then said, "You go back to Virginia City tonight, Jim, and I'll take care of things here."

Williams thought a second and then nodded. "I'm takin half the boys back to Virginia City with me. We got important business there to transact first thing tomorrow morning."

Later that night Beidler and six other men took Red Yeager down to a cottonwood tree by the creek. The temperature was about twenty-five below zero, and the wind howled, blew snow so hard against their faces it stung like tiny bits of ice. Beidler held up a lantern and cast a yellow light into the dark swirling night while his men got Red up on a stool and put the noose around his neck.

"X," Yeager cried, "I did what ya wanted. Just give me a chance to see those boys brought to justice, that's all I ask. It ain't fair, X, I told ya—"

Beidler kicked the stool out from under Yeager's feet. After a couple minutes he couldn't help but notice Yeager was still gasping for air, so he yanked down hard on his body to stop the damn gurgling.

Chapter Thirty-Four

Poor sonofabitch Red. Thought if he confessed, his confession would save him. Never reckoned just the opposite would happen, that his confession doomed him.

Jim Williams brought Red's confession to the next meeting of the Executive Committee in Virginia City, which was called right after Williams got back to town. Ten of the seventeen members of the Executive Committee got together in the same place, the back part of Pfouts's mercantile store, and among them were Wilbur Sanders, Paris Pfouts, Jim Williams, John Creighton, Neil Howie, X Beidler, John Lott, and two others. The meeting was secret, of course, but the deeds that came out of it were anything but secret.

I was lucky enough to hear afterward about the meeting from someone who was there and not sworn to secrecy. That was Colonel Sanders's little fifteen-year-old nephew, Henry Tilden. I got it straight from the horse's ass, you could say.

Tilden was there for one reason and one reason alone. Colonel Sanders had brought him along to testify against the sheriff. Several months earlier Tilden had told his Uncle a tall tale about being robbed by the sheriff and two other masked men while he was searching for a lost cow out on Horse Prairie Flat after dark. The robbers told him to stick his hands in the air and turn over all his money. When he emptied his pockets and showed he didn't have any, they rode away. His uncle asked how he knew it was Henry

Plummer, the sheriff. Well, he said, he saw the sheriff's pistol, and he also saw the red lining of the sheriff's coat. Didn't actually see the sheriff but saw his pistol and his coat.

Tilden also told me the same story later because I think what he'd said was bothering him. I asked why'd he tell it in the first place if he wasn't sure it was true. He answered by saying it might be true, and besides, it pleased his uncle to hear it. All he was doing was saying what his uncle wanted to hear; he didn't see any harm in that, at least to begin with, and once he'd said it, he couldn't change.

So Sanders brought Tilden to the meeting of the Executive Committee in Pfouts's store and had him sit in the back beyond the the vision and hearing of the other members. But in back where Henry Tilden sat, the room was freezing cold. So he slipped quietly past the counters of shirts and pants and pots and pans and got closer to the fire where he could warm his hands and feet. The heat from the stove warmed up the area where the executive committee sat in chairs in a circle. A couple of kerosene lamps sat on a table next to the stove and lit up the men's faces. His uncle Wilbur seemed to be in charge, the way he walked up and down in front of the other men.

What he heard Sanders say right away was, the sheriff was an obstacle to everything they wanted to do, to the very organization they had established. He stood in their way by refusing to banish the outlaws and renegades, even protecting them. The only way they were going to clean out the outlaws was to first clean out the sheriff himself.

Then Henry Tilden heard his uncle get real fierce about the sheriff. "He's a cold-blooded killer," the colonel said to the others, looking around with his jaw set hard. "I'd like to remind you men of Plummer's record back in California. That is, what really went on out there. First of all, our handsome sweet-talking sheriff shot a man down in cold blood after seducing his wife. That's a fact. The woman's name was Lucy Vedder, and there are court records to show it. Because of this murder, he served time in San Quentin prison with the worst dregs of humanity on the face of the earth.

Unfortunately, some folks in the Democrat Party in Nevada City got his sentence commuted because they had connections with the governor."

Sanders shook his head sadly. "After that, Plummer shot and killed an innocent young boy in a whorehouse brawl. Name of Riley. That's also in the record for anybody to see. Then he fled north to eastern Idaho where he got involved in more robbing and killing. After Idaho he came to Bannack, and practically the first thing he did was kill Jack Cleveland. That's his nature, gentlemen, to rob and kill. He's a killer."

Sanders stopped to let his words sink in. "Maybe I shouldn't say this, but there is talk now that Plummer is seducing his wife's sister, Martha Vail. That's right, Martha Vail. I won't go into that because it's gossip, but I wouldn't be a bit surprised if it turned out like the Vedder case in California, the sheriff killing her husband.

"Still, that's not the main thing to consider, gentlemen. You heard Yeager's confession from Jim here, that's down in black and white. Yeager was a witness. He swore Plummer was the leader of a gang of outlaws that robbed and killed countless innocent folks. I would wager over a hundred good men have been killed out on the roads and trails of this territory, murdered and never again heard from."

Then Sanders paused and said. "Now, to put the final touch on this case, I have another eyewitness to the misdeeds of our sheriff. It comes from my honest young nephew Henry Tilden, who was himself robbed by the sheriff."

Tilden was scared to death, of course—he told me so himself—but he testified anyway. It was too late to turn back, and besides that, his uncle Wilbur had told him exactly what to say.

"I was looking for a lost cow out on Horse Prairie one night and got stopped by these three fellas on horseback," he said. "One of 'em pulled out his pistol and said give up my money or he'd shoot me. Well, I just got paid for some chores I done and had about five dollars. I took it out and gave it to the man holding the pistol. He took it and asked if that's all I had. I turned my pockets inside out and said yessir. The reason I knew it was the sheriff is because I recognized the pistol and the red lining inside his coat."

Sanders broke in. "And then what did you do, Henry?"

Henry said, "I ran all he way home and told you, sir, what happened. And you told me not to tell anybody, and I didn't. Till now."

Nobody asked any questions after he testified, so Henry Tilden left the meeting and went back to the hotel where he was staying with his uncle.

So that's what happened. That's how the Executive Committee worked. They heard just one side.

Chapter Thirty-Five

Clubfoot George Lane came riding furiously into Bannack with the news from Virginia City. Limping into the sheriff's office dragging one foot, all out of breath, he said Red Yeager had been hanged by the vigilantes.

"Jim Williams and X Beidler was the ones done it."

The sheriff's face turned to stone. Normally he didn't show a thing in his face, but this time he looked like he was froze to death. I happened to be there slouching around his office that day because Crisman's store was the place folks gathered to talk gossip. One of the boys called it the news center for all of Bannack. It had a wide fireplace as well as the woodstove in Henry's office in the back. That day I didn't have anything else to do, because it was the first part of January, and the weather was so cold and the ground and creek so frozen that most of us didn't even try to work outside.

Right away the sheriff called in his deputies, Buck Stinson and Ned Ray, so they could also hear what Clubfoot George had to say. Trouble was, George didn't have much else to say. Only that Jim Williams and X Beidler were part of a gang of vigilantes who had hanged Red, that's all he knew. Had no inkling why. "Red was a cook," Clubfoot George said, "that's all he was, a goddamn cook. Worst thing he ever did was serve up his own grub."

This was the first time I ever saw the sheriff worried about something. He had already made it clear to everyone else in town he was dead set against the vigilantes. He hated them, especially after seeing those innocent men hanged back in California. "Worst thing you can do," he said, "is hang an innocent man."

It was a mystery, all right. He couldn't figure out why in God's name they'd hang someone like Red. "Jim Williams is taking orders, that much I know. So is X. But who's giving them orders? And why? I don't think we've seen the end of this, boys, not yet, anyway."

We were all sitting around the stove, and for a while nobody said a word; the room was dead silent. Then Henry asked, "What ya think, Buck? Folks don't like the way I'm running things?"

It was the first time I heard Henry say anything like that. Buck Stinson answered, "Folks in this town like you, Henry, leastwise the miners and ordinary folk do. That's most folks. I don't know about some of the churchgoin folks like Wilbur Sanders, who think their farts don't smell."

Buck shook his head. "I hear Sander's goin around town sayin we need a different kind of justice. But I don't reckon most folks agree with him. I'd say most folks side with you, Henry. You got elected, not him."

Henry stroked his chin with one hand. "He's a sonofabitch all right, but I don't take him for a murderin sonofabitch."

Ned Ray added, "I reckon there's always somebody like Wilbur Sanders around, fellas want to be in charge of everything, see things get done their way."

Henry said he was going over to talk to Sanders and Edgerton the next morning, Saturday, just to see what they knew. Meantime, he said, "We got to get organized, boys, in case those sonsabitches get it in their heads to come this way. I want you two, Buck and Ned, to round up fifteen or twenty fellas we can count on. Meet here Monday morning, and I'll swear 'em in. Put a stop to this foolishness before it goes any further."

Before the meeting was over, Henry went back to the hanging of Red Yeager. "Why in hell would they do it? What'd he done? Or what'd he know they wanted to know?" Nobody had an answer.

The next morning the sheriff paid a visit to Colonel Sanders and Judge Edgerton in Edgerton's log cabin. He told me later they were both friendly and invited him for a cup of coffee. When he asked what they knew about the vigilantes, they said they didn't know a thing, and furthermore, they didn't think he had to worry about them coming to Bannack because so many folks in town liked and respected him.

"All this'll pass, Henry, you'll see," Wilbur Sanders said with a grin.

The judge, Sidney Edgerton, added, "By my lights, these vigilantes just make the case more forcefully that we need a new territorial government out here to set things right. The boys in Congress are going to agree, I'd bet my bottom dollar."

Henry didn't like the sound of that, but he said nothing.

Meantime, the sheriff wasn't feeling well. Seemed like he was coming down with the grippe or something, and besides that he had a lot of other things to do. A couple of miners wanted him to come out to help them settle a claims dispute, and then there was a new problem raised by Dutch Wagner. Dutch Wagner had been captured after a botched robbery attempt of the Moody wagon train. He and another fella had tried to rob the stage and were so dumb that all they got out of it was being shot themselves. Neil Howie had brought Dutch back to Bannack and was holding him at his place. Henry didn't like the idea of Dutch being in the hands of Neil Howie, Howie playing like he was sheriff, so he had to get out there and talk to both Dutch and Neil.

What he needed most of all was a long stretch in bed.

Chapter Thirty-Six

Martha Vail had invited Henry Plummer and me to dinner Sunday night, telling us that since both of us were living by ourselves, we could use a home-cooked meal. I wondered if Martha had invited me so folks wouldn't talk about her inviting only Henry.

Anyway, Martha laid out a big spread of two roasted pheasants, a heaping bowl of steaming baked potatoes, a boat of gravy, a plate full of biscuits, and a dish of canned hominy. Those two pheasants just out of the oven gave off the sweetest smell in the world, which made my stomach start growling like a starved beast. I told Martha to put her ear down against my stomach and listen, but she just laughed.

I couldn't eat that damned hominy. I tried and almost threw up.

I sat next to the sheriff at the big wooden table in the kitchen—it always gave me a nice feeling sitting beside him—but that night he was ailing and hardly said a word. Martha was concerned about the vigilante talk and asked him what was happening. Henry said he had a meeting the next morning with a bunch of fellas to get organized. When he looked at Martha, her eyes lit up like she was surprised at something. I wondered if Martha's husband took notice. If he did, he didn't let on.

Still, Martha's raising the question of the vigilantes left a weird feeling in the air, as if everybody felt uneasy and didn't know what to say.

Just as dinner was over, we heard a loud knock on the door. Everybody looked around wondering who'd be out on a night like this in January with the temperature plunging way below zero. Turned out to be for the sheriff. He slipped into his heavy coat and said, "I'll be back in a few minutes, folks. The boys say Dutch John is making a confession I ought to hear."

After he was gone, Martha, who was ordinarily calm as bedrock, looked fidgety and worried. She said, "Why don't you go after him, Billy, see what's going on."

All bundled up against the cold, I left the cabin and started down the path where the men ahead had made tracks through the fluffy snow. I couldn't imagine why Martha was worried, though, or why me going after the sheriff would make her feel any better. Damn if it wasn't cold! Must of been at least thirty below that night, the air so dry and cold it froze the inside of my nose.

The tracks were easy to follow because the snow was about a foot deep on both sides of the trail. In only a couple minutes I spotted the men ahead of me, five of them, it looked like, standing in front of Wilbur Sanders's cabin. But the way they were standing there looked suspicious, four men in a circle around the sheriff. Then I made out four pistols pointed at the sheriff, and that sent a blast a fear through me.

I came up quietly from behind and heard the sheriff saying, "You put those guns away, boys, and we'll forget about this whole thing." But all four kept their pistols aimed right at him. My knees were shaking by this time. From where I stood, I recognized Jim Williams and Neil Howie. The sheriff kept talking, saying something about going over to the Goodrich for a drink before things went too far, before something happened everybody'd regret, and it seemed like he was succeeding. Jim Williams lowered his pistol and the others did likewise. Then I heard a man's voice shout, *"Attention, men!"*

It was Colonel Sanders striding down the path toward the group. Jim Williams jerked up his pistol. Henry watched the colonel swishing through the snow up the path and cried, "Wilbur, for God's sake, what's goin on here?"

Wilbur Sanders didn't even glance at the sheriff. He just called out, "Men, do your duty!" At this they prodded Henry around with their pistols, and the whole bunch tramped off down the path toward Main Street.

I didn't know what to do, so I followed along about ten paces back, shaking in my boots, my bare hands jammed in my pockets and clenched tight, scared to even think where they might be headed. The men could see me just as clearly as I could see them—Jim Williams peered right at me—but no one made a peep. They just turned their backs and tromped across the bridge over Grasshopper Creek out onto Main Street. The saloons were lit up in the distance, throwing yellow patches of light on the snow. I heard voices and laughter and the sound of fiddle music about a hundred paces down the street.

The sheriff kept turning his head and asking the colonel what was going on, why was he doing this anyway. "Goddammit, say something!" But Wilbur Sanders kept his mouth shut, and the men kept marching steadily across the road and out onto the flat north of town.

The sky was pitch dark that night except for a sliver of moon tipped up like a silver spoon in the east. The sound of the snow under the men's boots was a steady crunch, crunch, crunch, and I felt like I was going out of my mind. We entered the flat north of town where the land was covered by smooth snow except for the humps made by sagebrush underneath.

Up ahead I saw a group of men standing around in the light of torches, and behind them, looking in the torchlight like a cross in religious pictures, was what I feared most of all, the gallows. The same gallows Henry had used to hang Horan some months earlier. I had to swallow real hard in order not to scream.

A half dozen men in black coats and wide-brimmed hats were standing around the gallows, and soon I could make out two of them were prisoners, Buck Stinson and Ned Ray, the sheriff's deputies. When the men arrived at the gallows, Buck Stinson called out, "Say somethin to these fellas, Henry."

The sheriff tightened his face and turned again to the colonel. "For God's sake, Wilbur, at least tell us what we're charged with."

Everyone waited in silence while Sanders stood there straight as a lodgepole pine in his black overcoat and beaverskin hat. He sucked in his breath and said, "You've been sentenced to death by the Vigilance Committee of Virginia City, Henry Plummer, for being the leader of a murderous gang of outlaws."

I wanted to yell out that was a damn lie, but I stood there paralyzed right down to my toes.

The sheriff stared hard at Sanders. "I'm no leader of no gang of outlaws, and you know it, Wilbur." He turned and pointed at Buck Stinson and Ned Ray. "They supposed to be members of this gang of outlaws too?"

But Sanders paid no attention. He face was blank as snow. He turned to the men guarding Buck and Ned and said, "Men, do your duty!"

That's when I saw X Beidler. X stepped forward, fixed the noose around Ned Ray's neck, and tossed the rope over a beam some fifteen feet above. Ray was screaming that he was innocent, dammit, they was hangin' an innocent man. He shouted into X's face, "You murderin sonofabitch."

"That man's innocent, Wilbur!" the sheriff shouted.

Two men stepped up quickly beside Ray, each grabbed a leg and without a word tossed him into the air. Ray fell hard against the rope, but it didn't break his neck, and he grabbed at what was choking him to death. The sheriff shouted, *"For God's sake, X!"* Hearing this, the two men and X grabbed Ray's body and jerked him down hard in order to break his neck.

X called out, "Next!"

The two men brought Buck Stinson under the gallows, and Beidler fixed the noose. Dressed in his Sunday suit, Buck let go a long string of curses, then stopped and begged for a chance to say good-bye to his wife.

The two men looked at the colonel. Sanders shook his head, so they went ahead and did the same thing they'd done to Ned Ray, tossed him in the air. Only this time they gave Stinson a high enough drop so his neck broke.

Then X turned to Henry and said, "Your time has come, Sheriff." He grinned like the devil himself. Henry turned to Sanders and said, "Just give me till morning, Wilbur." His voice was wavering now, and I could tell he was holding everything down, not wanting to show he was scared. "I need to write to Electa," he said, "and my family back in Maine."

Hearing this I couldn't control myself any longer. I screamed and ran through the men toward Colonel Sanders, yelling for him to stop it, or leastwise wait till morning. But a man grabbed me by the arm and flung me to the snowy ground and held me there with both hands and his knee while I kicked and screamed. When I finished screaming, Sanders looked down at me lying on the ground and announced to everybody, "Nobody said God's work was easy, boys."

Henry saw me lying there and tore off his neckerchief and handed it to X Beidler. "Give this to Billy," he said. X just laughed and stuffed the neckerchief in his pocket. Then he grabbed Henry's arm and led him under the gallows and fixed the noose around his neck.

Henry turned to Sanders and said, "You know I've done nothing to deserve this, Wilbur."

Sanders stood straight with his shoulders back and his face still blank and cried, "Men, do your duty!"

Henry looked at the two boys who'd stepped forward to toss him in the air and said, "Gimme a high drop, boys." Those were his last words. He hit the end of the rope so hard, I felt the crack go through me like lightning.

BANNACK

I pounded my fists in the snow and cried and screamed for I don't know how long. After I stopped and looked around through blurred eyes, Colonel Sanders and the other men were still there. Sanders looked off into the distance, and there on the ridge of the hill about 50 yards away was the dark figure of Sidney Edgerton. Sidney Edgerton! A Supreme Court Judge for the territory of Idaho, watching the whole thing.

Chapter Thirty-Seven

YOU CAN GUESS HOW MUCH sleep I got that night. I lay in my bed staring up into the darkness and kept picturing Henry hanging there by the neck, couldn't get him out of my mind. Then I'd see Wilbur Sanders giving the order and Henry being lifted in the air, and, God Almighty, it was just awful, seeing those three bodies swinging there side by side in the torchlight. I tried to think of something else, but the hanging kept busting into my mind, and every time it did, I gritted my teeth and twisted my head and kicked my legs like I was going insane or something.

Well, it wasn't till near sunup I fell asleep, and then it didn't last long. I woke up about ten o'clock hearing gunfire outside. I jumped up and pulled on my overcoat and gloves and hat—I never even took off my clothes that night—and went out to see what was going on.

In the distance, on the side of the hill east of town, I saw a bunch of men milling around in front of Joe Pizanthia's cabin. The Greaser's place. It was a small cabin like mine, squatting up there by itself on the hill. The crazy thing was, several men gathered in front had their pistols drawn and were shooting into the wood door. Then my attention was knocked off to the left by another bunch of men pulling a small cannon up the hill by means of a rope. It was the brass cannon Judge Sidney Edgerton had acquired from the army as protection against the Indians, although there was no danger from the Indians. It just crouched there in front of his cabin next to the flag. A mountain howitzer it was called, and they were tugging and hauling it through the snow toward the Greaser's cabin.

I lit out fast as I could up the hill, wondering what in hell was going on. I couldn't imagine why anybody'd be after Joe Pizanthia.

By the time I got there, the men had wheeled the howitzer in place on the snowy slope and were aiming it straight at the cabin. I could hardly believe my eyes. A couple of the men aiming the cannon I recognized from the night before, part of the vigilante group led by Wilbur Sanders, but he wasn't there this time, nor was X Beidler or Jim Williams.

I was out of breath from running up the hill but grabbed the arm of someone I recognized and asked him what was happening. He said they was getting the Greaser because he was one of Henry Plummer's gang of outlaws. When I said, "That's crazy talk," he shrugged.

"Well, that's what the Vigilance Committee said, and I take what they say over the word of a Mexican can't even speak American."

It seemed like the world was coming undone all around me.

The man explained that the posse had earlier busted in the door of the Greaser's cabin, but instead of coming out like they ordered him to, he fired a shotgun from inside and hit Gordon Copley in the chest. Didn't look good for Copley, and now everyone was hopping mad. After firing at Copley, the Greaser slammed his door shut again.

By this time I saw they had the cannon loaded, and one man struck the fuse. The cannon exploded, and the ball crashed through one side of the cabin and blew through the other, leaving a gaping hole. A man near me shouted, "Ya dumb shit, John, ya forgot to cut the fuse." Meantime the fifteen or so men standing in front of the cabin started blazing away with pistols and rifles, zinging bullets through the hole caused by the cannonball and splintering wood where they missed.

The next shot from the howitzer was a bull's-eye. Somebody must have cut the fuse right, because the cannonball exploded as it hit the cabin and blew it to pieces. Sprawled out on the floor amid the rubble was Joe Pizanthia. Two men stepped in over the debris and dragged him out by the boots. I just stood there feeling helpless while they dragged the body down the hill through the snow toward Grasshopper Creek. Looked to me like poor Joe was still alive, the way his arms were flopping, but I couldn't tell for sure. I slipped and skidded down the hill after the whole bunch, wondering why these fellas were taking orders from the Vigilance Committee. Seemed like most of these men were quality citizens gone crazy.

When we got to the creek, the men strung Joe up by the feet from the limb of a cottonwood. Then the whole bunch of them started firing into his body with pistols, rifles, and shotguns as fast at they could, loading and reloading, whooping while they fired. Joe's body jumped and shook and danced and twisted as the bullets hit from all sides.

The men got so damn excited shooting at the Greaser's body, they even hit two of their own. That stopped them, at least. Made me glad to see the bastards get hit.

After that, I scrambled back to the Goodrich to get some breakfast, even though I wasn't hungry. As I walked up the steps of the hotel, I was horrified to see the bodies of Henry and his two deputies lying out on the porch, frozen stiff. Jesus, I had to turn my head away as I walked by, thinking, *How could the vigilantes do this?* These men weren't outlaws, leastwise to my knowledge. There wasn't even any gang of outlaws, to my knowledge. How could Henry be head of a gang that didn't exist?

I sat down at a table in the saloon and ordered steak and biscuits and coffee but couldn't eat a thing. I drank coffee and stared at the wall. Bill Goodrich came in carrying a pearl-handled shotgun I recognized as Henry's. He held it up proudly and said he got it from Henry's office. The sonofabitch! Then suddenly it dawned on me that nearly half my money was in the sheriff's safe over at Crisman's store. Seven hundred dollars. I'd cached seven hundred dollars in that safe. I jumped up quickly and ran over to see if it was still there. It wasn't.

Francis Thompson was there and told me the safe and everything in it had been carted away by the vigilantes. Nearly half my savings gone. I still had another nine hundred in the Goodrich safe, thank God, but that wasn't much to cheer about. Then it crossed my mind that they also got everything Henry had in the safe, everything, and that was a lot more than what I had there.

Chapter Thirty-Eight

I THREW MYSELF HEADLONG INTO THE everlasting arms of Al K. Hall, what Boone called man's best friend up here in this godforsaken wilderness.

The picture of Henry hanging from the gallows haunted me off and on all day long and into the night. The more I saw it, the more I drank. One night I broke down and cried myself to sleep. I must have drunk a barrel of Barleycorn in the week after Henry's death.

The thing about drinking was how easy and cheap it was. A sack a flower cost thirty dollars, while a gallon of Valley tan cost four or five. Add in some chewing tobacco at seven dollars a pound, and a man could stay drunk a whole month for under forty dollars.

The more I drank, though, the worse I felt. One night I dreamed I was back at the hospital in St. Louis, lying on a stretcher in the operating tent, and two men hoisted me up on a table in front of Wendell Milliken, who had a butcher knife in one hand and a fiendish grin on his face. When he leaned over to carve my leg off, I woke up, thank God. The more I drank, the worse my dreams got. But you think that cured me? Not a bit. I kept right on drinking, even as I got sick unto death.

I did a lot of complaining about the vigilantes and wasn't alone either. Several other fellas who drank with me in the Goodrich saloon cursed them out as pot-licking, shit-eating, self-righteous murdering sonsabitches. But we did this bitching mostly among ourselves, in the private space of the Goodrich.

It wasn't that ordinary folks in Bannack liked the vigilantes either, especially the secret way they operated, never giving a man a chance to defend himself. Several folks told me in private they knew Henry was innocent, even felt sorry for him, but they didn't want to say it very loudly; they were scared what the vigilantes might do. Folks bent the way the wind blew, I guess, and right then it was blowing from the vigilantes. Being safe won out over being truthful.

One exception to this chicken-hearted quiet was a man named Rawley. RC, we called him. He was a harmless old fart who had no feet. What happened to his feet was the same thing happened to Ding-Dong Bell. RC left them out of his bed one night while he was dead drunk and woke up the next morning looking at a couple of black rocks. Didn't hurt, he said, but they didn't move either. After everything else failed, Doc Bissell amputated both feet, and RC fashioned a couple of pegs to walk on. He drank even more whiskey after that and got even louder with his opinions. One night he stood right out in the street and shouted, "I say the vigilantes are a bunch o' murderin, stranglin fiends."

Next morning someone pounded on the door of my cabin and shouted to come see what happened. So I plodded down Main Street on the hard-packed snow to the south end of town, and there was RC hanging from the beam of a corral, his head wrenched up to one side, his tongue sticking out the side of his mouth, his face twisted in eternal pain. Two bones instead of pegs stuck out the bottom of his trousers.

A crowd had gathered, and everyone was pointing to how the hangmen had torn his coat in front and back and ripped his pants in six different places. Everyone knew that meant the vigilantes had done it. RC was a warning message to everyone there. And everyone heard it.

All this time I was drinking, the Elkhorn was closed. Cyrus Skinner cut out of town after hearing his name was on the vigilante list of outlaws, thinking that if he put a couple hundred miles distance between himself and the vigilantes, he'd be safe. He didn't count on the grit of men who thought they were doing God's work. They tracked him down in Hellgate and hanged him.

Same with most of the others, too. In the next week or two the blood-soaked bastards caught up with and hanged over fifteen men on Red's list. X came into the Goodrich saloon some nights afterward and bragged about it. "We'll get 'em all before the month's out, mark my words." Didn't matter that every single one of those fellas claimed they were innocent right to the end. X paid no heed. "Shit, it don't matter what they say, that's just a code word they use. I'm innocent."

One question kept going over and over in my mind: where were Boone and Jack? Last I heard they were heading for Virginia City, right into the jaws of the beast, but that's all I knew. I crossed my fingers and hoped they got the hell out of town before it was too late.

During this awful time I got a letter from Harriet saying she was fine, the baby was fine, and she was going back to St. Louis as soon as the river was open to the steamboats. That gave me a jolt, thinking about her returning to St. Louis. Made me wonder if I should go too.

Then came another shocker. I was sitting in Crisman's store in front of his wide fireplace, talking with several other fellas, when a man named Charley Forbes came rushing in all out of breath and said, "Listen to this, boys, the vigilantes done captured Boone Helm and Jack Gallagher. That's right, Boone and Jack. They're over in Leviathan Hall in Virginia City, along with Haze Lyons, Frank Parish and Clubfoot George Lane."

Chapter Thirty-Nine

NO MISTAKING, THERE WAS GOING to be hanging that day. Besides the folks from Virginia City, others had come to town from the nearby mining camps of Summit, Nevada, Alder Gulch, and You Bet. Hundreds of people milled around, moving in the same direction, some men on horseback but most on foot, kids skipping around their slower moving folks, women in their heavy coats and shovel hats. A man beside me said five thousand people had come to town to see the show.

It felt like a Fourth of July parade back in Ada.

It was also a sunshiny day, and the sky was icy blue, one of those cold winter days when the sun takes some of the bite out of the air. I saw a couple of men walking along without coats, even though it was still about zero degrees.

As we came closer to the show, the crowds got denser, and people started pushing and shoving and craning their necks to see. I reckoned there was no way I'd see anything from where I stood way back in the crowd, so I slipped over to a side street, circled around behind the stores facing the street, climbed over a wood fence and skipped through the yard of a house till I came up behind a frame building, which I guessed was across the street from the hanging place. I got atop a wood box and pulled myself up to the edge of the roof and threw my legs over. Lucky for me it was a flat roof. I walked across the roof to one of those fake storefronts and leaned over the edge to look. Damned if I wasn't right where I'd calculated.

On the other side of the street from me was what I dreaded to see, an unfinished frame building with no roof or sides yet, just a skeleton of a building, but with a large crossbeam in front and five ropes dangling down, nooses at the end of each. Under each noose was a big wood crate that sat at least three feet high. Goddamn if it didn't give me a shiver.

I kept telling myself Boone and Jack were going to find a way out of this, they always had before, but the fear in me was so powerful, it was drowning out all hope. A clutch of young boys down on the street saw me up on the roof and started talking among themselves and pointing up. Wasn't long before I had company, five other boys leaning over the storefront and looking out above the mob of people backed up the streets for a block or more.

After another few minutes, I finally saw what I was dreading to see. A short column of men in dark coats and wide-brimmed hats carrying rifles on their shoulders marched down the street through the crowd, the people falling away to both sides as if this was a parting of the Red Sea. Right up front were Wilbur Sanders, Paris Pfouts, and Jim Williams. Behind them, surrounded by armed men, came the five prisoners: Boone and Jack, limping Clubfoot George, Haze Lyons, and Frank Parish. X Beidler, the hangman, was walking right beside the prisoners and saying something to them. Their hands were tied behind their backs.

The whole bunch marched right up to the frame house and stopped. X broke through the men first, stepped out onto the floor of the house, and stood at attention.

Behind X the prisoners were escorted up onto the floor of the building, each one forced to stop beside one of the wood crates. Boone and Jack were the last two in line. The way they were lined up, Jack was probably the first to go, then Boone. Jack had on his long gray Confederate cavalry coat unbuttoned and hanging loose in front. Boone was dressed in his dark overcoat and hatless, his scraggly hair falling down on all sides except the front. His beard was trimmed as if he'd cut it for the occasion. First time I ever saw him with a trimmed beard.

All five prisoners stood in a row facing the crowd, each with a guard standing to one side. They all looked straight ahead and grim except for Boone, who searched around the crowd for people he knew. He spotted me sitting up on the roof across the way and shouted, "Hey there, Billy boy, I see ya come to the party." I waved back, but I was starting to feel sick to my stomach too. Jack looked up at me and nodded hello. I could see he was scared even from that distance. I raised my hand again, but it felt kind of funny waving.

Boone then spotted a lady in the crowd and cried, "Hey there, lady, you're lookin mighty pretty today." She looked embarrassed but smiled back anyway. Boone added, "I'll be there to hold open the pearly gates for ya, honey."

Colonel Sanders strode out in front of the prisoners and turned to the crowd. "The Viligance Committee of Virginia City has found these men guilty of being members of a murderous gang of outlaws. They have therefore been sentenced to hang by the neck until they are dead." Then he swung about and said, "Men, do your duty."

Each prisoner was forced up onto his wood crate, and his guard fitted the noose around his neck. (Later someone asked X if he didn't feel anything for those men he hanged, and he said, "Hell, yes, I feel somethin, I feel for their right ear.") Clubfoot George was crying and slobbering that he was innocent, which he was. One of the guards had slipped a hood over Frank Parish's face before he fitted the noose around his neck. Haze Lyons was praying, mumbling something I couldn't hear, and his eyes lifted to the sky. Jack was saying something to Boone that made Boone laugh.

"Gimme a drink o' whiskey before I go," Boone shouted.

Sanders looked discomfited at that, but someone in the crowd yelled, "Give it to him, for God's sake." So Sanders signaled someone to fetch whiskey.

X stood up on the box next to Boone and poured half a bottle of whiskey into his mouth and all over his face. Boone had his mouth wide open gulping down as much as he could, then he spit some into X's face. "I'll see you in hell, X," he cried, "you murderin, no-good sonofabitch." Then he turned to the crowd and shouted, "How do I look, folks, this halter round my neck?"

Some men in the crowd laughed, but not loud. I felt a lump in my throat.

Colonel Sanders then cried out again those words he seemed to like so much, words I'll never forget: "Men, do your duty!"

Jack Gallagher looked up at me and nodded and then turned to Boone and said something I couldn't hear but from his lips looked like, "So long, you no-good old bastard." Jack was laughing and crying at the same time when X kicked the crate out from under him. He fell about two feet but his neck didn't break, and he kicked and squirmed.

Boone called after him, "Kick away, old buddy, I'll be with ya in no time."

Before X got to him, Boone glared at Sanders and cried, "Ya stranglin sonofabitch, I hope forked lightnin strikes yer black heart." Then he shot his eyes over at me and yelled, "Stick to yer principles, Billy. I'm goin to a worse climate, but I'm goin in good company." With that he jumped as high as he could into the air, and I jerked my head around because I couldn't watch him hit the end of the rope. I turned quickly and ran off the roof as fast as I could and snaked my way through the crowds back to the hotel. I threw myself on my bed and lay there for a long time. It felt like I was dead. Didn't think anything, just lay there numb and paralyzed.

Chapter Forty

I knew Martha had taken the death of Henry hard, maybe even harder than I had. Her husband James told me she'd fainted dead away when she heard Henry was hanged. I believe she loved Henry as much as Electa did.

Even so, I'd put off going to see her until my conscience finally kept me awake at night, accusing me of being chicken, screaming at me to do the right thing and see her.

It was another one of those cold, blustery days in January when I got to her place. We sat down for a cup of coffee, and she said right away she was feeling better and appreciated me stopping by. After asking about me, she said she'd written a long letter to Electa but hadn't heard back yet. She knew Electa was going to be terribly distressed. It'd take her a long time to get over Henry's death, especially since she wasn't here, but eventually she'd have to, because that's what life did: it slapped you in the face so hard you had to cry, but never so hard you couldn't recover.

She talked of the good times they had together, the four of them, Henry and Electa, Martha and James, and she got pretty weepy about it. After a while she put her head on my shoulder and started crying so hard her whole body shook. I patted her on the back and pulled her head hard against my chest and held her there. I had to bite down with all my might to keep from coming undone myself.

She didn't know what they were going to do now, her and James and the two children. They'd heard of a homestead that was available, and perhaps they'd move, but she wasn't sure. It was hard to think of anything. She asked me what I was going to do, and I told her I didn't know either.

Before I left that day, Martha said she'd heard that over in Virginia City there was a man named Thomas Dimsdale who had just become editor of a brand-new newspaper, and he was going to write a story about the vigilantes for the history books. "You ought to go over there and talk to him, Billy. Tell Mr. Dimsdale what you knew about Henry, just so he'll hear Henry's side of things."

I had heard of Mr. Dimsdale, and what I'd heard was, he was a friend of Wilbur Sanders. That made me think going over to see him was no use, but when I told Martha this, she said maybe so, but I should go anyway, it wouldn't hurt.

"I'll think on it, Martha," I said before I left.

Before I could make up my mind to visit Thomas Dimsdale, I was out walking one sunny day and came across a little ceremony to celebrate the departure of Wilbur Sanders and Sidney Edgerton for Washington. It took place in front of the Goodrich Hotel, and most of the merchants were there to say good-bye and wish them Godspeed. I noticed none of the miners or common folks in attendance. Sanders and Edgerton were setting off on horseback for Salt Lake City, from where they planned to take the stage to St. Louis and the train to Washington DC.

Edgerton gave a little speech while he sat his horse, ready to leave. He said the boys in Washington were going to listen to him because he had what it took to make a Congressman listen. Saying this, he patted his overcoat, which didn't mean anything to me until Francis Thompson told me later he was referring to a small treasure in gold that had been sewed into the coat. Furthermore, Edgerton said, he had heard from his friends in Congress that they were disposed to do what he requested of them, namely pass a law creating a new territory, with Bannack as the capital. He had even heard a name mentioned for the new territory: Montana. He didn't much like the name, it wasn't Anglo-Saxon enough for his taste, but he'd take it if that's what the boys in Congress wanted. Land of the shining mountains. Montana.

Francis Thompson, who was there explaining things to me that morning, said the trip was bought and paid for by the Vigilance Committee of Virginia City. So when they rode off together, the colonel and the judge, I thought, *There goes nearly half my money, and all of Henry's.* I didn't much like the idea of paying for their trip, I doubted it was going to do me any good, but what choice did I have?

Chapter Forty-One

I walked into Thomas Dimsdale's office in Virginia City and introduced myself as a young man desirous of becoming a newspaper writer. That got his attention right away. I told him I didn't need any pay to begin with because I'd work free if he'd learn me the trade.

"Teach me," he corrected. Those were his first words, "Teach me." He spoke with an English accent, and I could see he was a man strong on being correct.

Folks said Dimsdale had come to America fifteen years earlier, after running away from some scandal in England. He became a schoolteacher in America and moved out west to cure a lung disease, consumption, someone said. I didn't know if it was lung disease or if he was just skinny, but he had a caved-in chest and a body so frail it looked like a strong breeze'd blow him away.

He pushed the spectacles back on his long nose and said, "I like to hear a boy speak out boldly, it shows character. What I'm going to do," he said, "is start you immediately on the task of cleaning up the office."

So the first week I worked hard getting everything spick-and-span. His office wasn't big, just a small store on Wallace Street with the machinery in back and a desk and chairs up front. I cleaned everything in sight, including the printing press and type drawers and stuff like that in the rear. All the while I watched him working on his story about the vigilantes and one night asked if I could read what he was writing. I was scared he'd say no, but he didn't. He declared he was "delighted" to show me what he'd written because in his humble opinion "this is going to be the official record of what happened."

So that's how I got to read Mr. Dimsdale's newspaper stories about the vigilantes. It wasn't easy reading, either, because I found there were so many lies in his writing, I had to force myself to keep going and not tear the papers to pieces.

For instance, Mr. Dimsdale declared right at the start that there had been a villainous gang of outlaws around Bannack and Virginia City, and these outlaws robbed and murdered over a hundred people under the orders of a fiend named Henry Plummer who masqueraded as the sheriff of Bannack by day while being an outlaw at night.

I had to read that particular section twice. Over a hundred people robbed and murdered. I knew I could prove that wasn't true. I could tell Mr. Dimsdale I had been a friend of the sheriff all summer and fall and knew who'd got robbed and killed, and it certainly wasn't a hundred people. To begin with, there were only three big robberies during all that time: the Peabody stage, the Oliver stage, and the MacGruder pack train. The Moody wagon train was stopped but never really robbed.

As for murders, I reckoned five fellas had been killed on the Magruder pack train, but that was over in western Idaho, done by outlaws over there, way outside the jurisdiction of the sheriff. No one was murdered from the other two robberies. So all told, counting Nick Tiebolt, there were six men killed in robberies during the whole time Henry was sheriff. Six, and five didn't count. You could say a seventh was George Evans, but he was killed by Jack Cleveland before Henry became sheriff. Of course some other fellas died, like Horan, Banfield, Carrhart, and Bell, but they got killed for different reasons, fighting or freezing, that had nothing to do with the law.

So I'd tell Mr. Dimsdale the facts.

JERRY DELANEY

That wasn't all, though. I had to grit my teeth reading the rest of what Mr. Dimsdale wrote. The worst thing was about the hanging itself. He wrote that when Henry was faced with the gallows, he confessed his guilt and got down on his knees and cried and declared to God he was "too wicked" to die. Seeing that, I nearly threw the pages in the fire, because I'd been there, and I knew for a fact what happened. A coward was the last thing Henry Plummer was.

I couldn't help wondering why Dimsdale would write stuff like that. He wasn't even there. Somebody must have told him what to say. Then I remembered what Colonel Sanders had said in his speech to the Executive Committee: that over a hundred innocent men had been murdered. I reckoned that's where Mr. Dimsdale must have got his information, from Colonel Sanders. No one else ever said such a crazy thing.

Some of the other stuff Mr. Dimsdale wrote was even crazier, for instance that all the gang members wore a mustache and chin whiskers and used the word "innocent" as a code word so they would recognize each other. Made no goddamn sense at all, except I remember X saying something just like that. They must have agreed on what to say.

I stacked up the papers in a pile on Mr. Dimsdale's desk and went back to my hotel for the night. Next day I watched for my chance. After Mr. Dimsdale had finished his morning writing and was commencing on his lunch, I slipped over and sat down. We sat across from each other in front of the iron stove in his office. I told him I'd read his articles and asked if he would kindly listen to what I had to say.

He said, "Of course I will, Billy." He tipped his head back and stared at me through his spectacles.

I didn't beat around the bush. I said his facts were plain wrong about a gang a villainous outlaws and a hundred people being killed. Then I told him why I knew they were wrong and why I knew the sheriff was no leader of any gang.

He didn't say anything for a long time. Then he looked at me and said there were things I didn't understand because of my age and lack of knowledge. What I didn't understand, above all, was the importance of making sure everybody thought the vigilantes did the right thing. That was his job, to make sure everybody understood the vigilantes acted out of rightness.

He gave me a serious look. "Sometimes," he said, "you have to arrange the facts like flowers so folks will see the deeper truth."

I reared back at this. "How can it be the right thing to hang a man," I said, "if the things you said he did to deserve hanging ain't true?"

Dimsdale shook his head as if something was sadly wrong with me. "Forget about the sheriff, Billy; he's gone. He chose the wrong side in this war against evil, protecting those no-good roughs like he did. It was his own fault he got hanged. As for us, you and me, we are standing before the bar of History, and our solemn task is to make certain the vigilantes are judged as having done the right thing."

"But what you say isn't true, Mr. Dimsdale."

He got terribly upset at that. "I'm not going to argue with you, Billy. I'll say this one last time: You don't understand. You just don't understand that our first obligation is to be loyal to our friends. Loyalty in the cause of what's right is more important than truth in the cause of evil. Besides, we've got to be an inspiration to the young, that's our task."

"That still don't make sense to me, Mr. Dimsdale, what's right being different from what's true."

I could see the red rise in his face now. He had finished his lunch of steak and biscuits and coffee, and he carefully wiped off his mouth with his handkerchief as if he wanted to keep himself under control. "We're fighting a war, Billy! Henry Plummer and those cutthroats were a threat to the peace and security of our community. As Colonel Sanders said, once you identify the enemy, you must do whatever it takes, even if that means acting without mercy."

I started to say something, but he raised his hand. "I've heard quite enough from you, Billy. Now let me give you some advice. Don't go saying what you just said outside this office, or you're going to get yourself in deep trouble. I wouldn't want to see you get hurt."

I was so hopping mad I banged my fist on his desk, jumped up, knocking over my chair, stomped out, and slammed the door behind me.

Chapter Forty-Two

walked up Wallace Street without noticing the horses and buggies and folks around me. My head was spinning, and I couldn't think straight. Without knowing where I was going, I cut onto a narrow dirt road that led up a steep hill north of town. I needed to walk, get into the clean air and away from the lying town. My insides were roiling from all the lies. Lies and more lies. Henry and the boys being hanged because of lies. Dimsdale even making history a lie.

My jaw was sore from biting down so hard.

After a while I found myself on top of a high hill overlooking Alder Gulch and the town of Virginia City. The gulch cut a deep crease down the side of the mountain, and the town ran alongside the crease. To the north I saw the snow-covered peaks of the Tobacco Mountains, gleaming white against the blue sky. To my other side, about fifty yards off, I noticed five graves lined up in a row, out there all by themselves on this bench of land. I didn't know whose graves they were, but I had a funny feeling in my belly.

I walked over. The snow covered all five, but each made a slight mound, showing where the men had been buried. Someone had nailed two wood planks together and drove them in the ground at the head of each grave. Written on the wood planks were the names: George Lane, Frank Parish, Haze Lyons, Boone Helm, Jack

Gallagher. On each grave marker were the same words: Hanged, January 14, 1864.

I stood there a long time just looking and feeling queasy inside. I knew nobody was going to feel sorry for those fellas, especially Boone and Jack. They were hard-drinking, shiftless, no-good, low-life drifters who didn't give a damn about anybody but themselves. You could say they were a disgrace to the human race. But I knew in my heart they weren't murderers. I couldn't imagine Boone or Jack as murdering outlaws. The only people they really hurt was themselves.

"Goin to a warmer climate," Boone had said. A warmer climate! He could even joke about hell. I reckoned he could joke about it because he didn't really believe in hell. He'd said it was made up by the preachers to keep folks in line. The more I thought about it, the more old Boone made sense to me. Just considering him and Jack down there burning in fire and brimstone for eternity made no sense. Unless they were throwing insults at the devil himself, calling him a damn poor excuse for a badman.

Then it crossed my mind that maybe that's what I was going to take from Boone, not believing in hell. He was surefire proof there was no hell.

Anyway, I'd miss their low-life company.

Wilbur Sanders, though, he was something else. That sonofabitch believed in hell all right. He even took hell out of his own mind and put it on earth so everybody else could feel it. Sanders was not a hell-raiser, he was a hell-maker, and that was worse. My pa believed in hell too, although he wasn't so bad as Sanders about it. Next time I saw Pa, I was gonna say he'd be a damn sight better off if he'd stop believing in hell and start living a little more.

I stood there a long time, looking at the graves lying peaceful and quiet up there in the land of the shining mountains.

Of the whole bunch, though, I'd remember Henry Plummer best because I admired and loved him the most. There was a hard side to Henry—he made some big mistakes, getting himself into scrapes he should have stayed away from, in California especially—but he was a decent man, and he was fair with folks, tried to help others where he could, and he had a philosophy that had a kindness in it. That's what I'd remember most about Henry, I reckoned, his idea of giving folks a little slack, live and let live.

    A bite of cold wind jolted me, and I started down the hill toward town. As I trudged through the snow, I thought that for the past couple weeks I'd been telling myself there was nothing I could do about what was happening. Well, maybe there wasn't anything I could do to change things, but it wasn't written down anywhere that I had to continue living in the midst of all these lies. I sure as hell didn't want to live in Thomas Dimsdale's history. I reckoned the road to liberty didn't end in a country where people were scared of hearing the truth.

Epilogue

When I got aboard the steamboat, Harriet was already there waiting. Eleven months since we'd seen each other, and at first she didn't look as good as the person I had in mind while jacking off in my hanky. Didn't matter, though. Remember, Harriet was one of those girls who got better looking the more you got to know her.

Because the steamboat was going with the current instead of against it, the trip back to St. Louis was a lot faster than the one coming up. Two weeks compared to four.

We did a lot of walking and talking and staring at the muddy river in those two weeks. Harriet said it was distressing to leave the baby, but once she'd set her mind to getting back to St. Louis and beginning her own business, making a new life for herself, she was getting over it. Her plans were to open a fur shop and be a businesswoman, receiving furs from her uncle's trading company.

Her eyes lit up, and her face got lively when she talked, and I couldn't stop myself from being drawn to her. She was like a magnet; I gravitated to her.

She thought I ought to go to college in St. Louis and said she'd find a place for me if I did. She'd even find a job for me in her fur shop if everything worked out like she planned it. But I shied from that. I still had nearly nine hundred dollars cached away in my money belt, which was not as much as I had dreamed of making, but it wasn't bad either, and it gave me the feeling I was free to do what I wanted, and what I wanted wasn't college, least not yet.

I had my seventeenth birthday on the boat, and we sat out on the deck holding hands and talking till late at night. I kissed her and suggested we celebrate my birthday by having sexual intercourse. Harriet laughed and said she'd like to do it, but she was afraid of getting pregnant again. So what we did was go down in the hold and find a dark corner where we could lie in the hay meant for the mules and kiss and touch without witnesses. Harriet wasn't bashful about giving me pleasure. She took hold of the boss like he was an old friend, and she even showed me how to touch her between the legs with my middle finger. Best birthday present I ever got, learning to give pleasure as well as take it.

Before I had a chance to get bored, we were in St. Louis and saying good-bye to each other. Leaving Harriet stung all right; I thought the world of her, but we both knew we were too young to get married and settle down, and I didn't know what in the world I wanted to do anyway. So we hugged and kissed and promised to keep in touch with each other. I had a strong feeling I would see her again one day.

I visited Mrs. Rhinehart, and she was so excited to see me she got tears in her eyes. But I couldn't wait to get home and promised her I'd get in touch when I got back to St. Louis the next time.

I took the stage from St. Louis to my home town of Ada and walked out to the farm, arriving in the late afternoon just before supper. When I walked in, the whole family except Mama was in the living room, and they looked up like they'd seen a ghost. "Billy!" my sisters shouted, all four running up and jumping all over me. Pa put the paper down and just stared, didn't say a word or move a muscle. Mama walked out from the kitchen wiping her hands on her apron and stopped in her tracks. It looked like she had tears in her eyes, although I couldn't be sure.

Finally Pa got up and strode over to shake hands, and I handed over the hundred and fifty dollars I owed him. "I'm ready to let bygones be bygones," he muttered under his breath, as if he didn't want anybody else to hear him say it. He turned back to Mama and said, "You're lookin at the story of the prodigal son, Mama."

"Nonsense," she said softly, never passing up a chance to take a swipe at Pa's religious talk.

'Course everybody wanted to know about my trip, and I told them the whole story at dinner that night. I never talked so much without stopping in my life. Then, after dinner, everyone wanted to know what I was going to do next.

Pa said I ought to join the army and fight for the Union cause. But that was one thing I knew I didn't want to do. I said I had no intention of adding to the pile of bodies that Abraham Lincoln was going to stand on to proclaim victory. "It's too high as it is."

Pa didn't like that kind of talk. I could see the muscles twitch as he bit down on his jaw, but he held his tongue.

It wasn't till the next day that Mama and I had a chance to visit, just the two of us. She invited me into her library, and we sat down side by side on her reading couch. She didn't say a word for a while, just sat there in silence with her hands folded in her lap, her shoulders back and her hair combed smooth and tidy. Then, gazing into my eyes, she said, "Well, what have you learned, Billy Mayfair?" Then she laughed and said how glad she was to see me again. She kept right on gazing too, and there was so much affection pouring out, I felt the skin on my arms tingle. She was doing with her eyes what she never allowed herself to do with words.

"What I'm wondering, Billy, is what you're planning to do with yourself next."

Up till then I had no idea what to say. Then all of a sudden it came to me: I wanted to do what that soldier boy in the Army hospital, Harold Boykin, had said he wanted to do after he got out. "I'm setting off to see the world, Mama. I'd like to find out how other people live."

She nodded her head as if she knew this all along. Then she said, "There's a whole ocean of solitude out there, you know. Searching like that doesn't come free of loneliness and pain." I nodded and said it didn't matter. She slid over on the couch and gave me a hug like

I'd never had from her before, her head laid against my shoulder, her fingers clutched into my back, a shudder going through her body.

"I never told you this before, Billy, but I would have liked to do that too, when I was your age. My father had the money, but I was always too much afraid of being alone, being alone and being a woman both. I'm mighty proud of you."

Those words struck me right in the heart.

When I told Pa that I was going to set out to see the world, he just frowned and shook his head. "You're takin an awful chance, Billy, havin intercourse with them folks that don't have the same religion and don't have the same loyalties. Might be a big mistake."

"I'm not scared of making a mistake, Pa."

Two days later I rode the stage to Springfield, where I got the train to the East Coast and Baltimore. I'd read in the newspapers that Baltimore was the place where a fleet of packets sailed regular for Liverpool, England. I'd never ridden on a train before, so it was a thrill to sit by the window staring out at the countryside; that ride gave me a lot of time to ponder things.

I took notice how the countryside was showing all the marks of springtime, long rows of green shoots popping up in the dark soil, thick woods greening the boundaries of the planted fields, white farmhouses here and there on the land, smoke rising from the chimneys.

Mainly I just sat in my seat by the window and daydreamed. I had to smile when I thought about Mama and Pa, how different they were. Pa wanted me to get ready for dying, while Mama wanted me to get ready for living. Everything she taught me over the years, all the books she baited me to read, all that poking fun at the preacher, all that sly laughing at Pa's strict religion, all the times she stood up for me against Pa's senseless wrath, shielded me from his scorn, coaxed me to stand on my own two legs, use my imagination, hold to the idea that a life lived as adventure was better than a life lived at home doing ordinary things—everything she did was getting me ready to do what I was doing right at that moment. I had to smile all right, smile and bite down real hard.

Afterword

HERE IS WHAT ACTUALLY HAPPENED to some of the leading characters in our story:

Henry Plummer was buried in a shallow grave near the gallows in Bannack. In later years his bones were dug up by vandals and, for the most part, lost somewhere in the anonymous landscape of southwestern Montana. Except apparently for his skull, which was acquired by a barkeep in Bannack and put on display behind the bar of his Bank Exchange Saloon as a conversation piece. One night the saloon burned to the ground, and the last remnant of the sheriff vanished. No trace of Henry Plummer remains except his reputation as the most notorious outlaw in Montana history.

Electa was of course grief-stricken at the news of Henry's death. Although she refused to talk about the subject, most folks think she believed deeply in his innocence to the end of her life. Electa received none of Plummer's rich assets; they were no doubt confiscated and used by the vigilantes, as they claimed it was their right to do. After ten years of mourning, Electa married a widower with six children and had three sons of her own. She died three days before her seventieth birthday, remembered in history as the wife of a famous outlaw.

Martha Vail and her husband James moved out of Bannack shortly after Henry was hanged. After another abortive attempt at working the Sun River farm and an inglorious attempt at homesteading in South Dakota, they returned to Ohio. Martha had a child called Rena whom some folks said was the fruit of her romance with Henry Plummer. There is no reliable evidence to substantiate this rumor. Martha's husband James died at the age of forty-four, and she devoted the remainder of her life to supervising a home for orphans.

Thomas Dimsdale was awarded a set of silver pistols by the vigilantes after his series of articles on the vigilantes appeared. Governor Sidney Edgerton appointed him Superintendent of Public Instruction. A distinguished journalism award is now given in his name.

Sidney Edgerton was a miserable failure as governor. After one year in office he aroused so much antagonism vis-à-vis the legislature that the machinery of government was brought to a standstill. He resigned abruptly and fled into retirement with seventy-five lucrative mining claims in hand. My best guess is that he got these claims in exchange for granting licenses for toll roads and bridges. In any case, he acquired enough money as governor to buy a prosperous farm in Ohio and live out his life in ease.

Jim Williams is said to have become depressed in later years, haunted, some say, by the specter of so many innocent men hanging from the gallows. On a cold winter day in a grove of fir trees on his farm, Williams committed suicide by taking an overdose of laudanum. His body was found the next day frozen solid.

X Beidler worked as a lawman in Montana for many years after his vigilante heroics. He is portrayed by some senseless historians as a "picturesque character." He died in 1890 and was buried beneath a gravestone that proclaimed, "Public Benefactor, Brave Pioneer, To True Occasion True."

Boone Helm and Jack Gallagher lie in clearly marked graves on Boot Hill outside Virginia City. Although some have tried to make up stories about them, the truth is, little is actually known about their lives except they were low-life roughs hanged by the vigilantes. Only someone like Billy Mayfair would find them suitable companions.

BANNACK

Wilbur Sanders was highly successful in Montana politics. He became known as Mr. Republican, famous for his slashing tongue and scorched-earth rhetoric. He was appointed by the legislature in 1890 as the state's first United States Senator. His larger-than-life bronze statue now stands proudly on the lawn of the state capital at Helena, adorned in frock coat and tie, ramrod straight, gazing outward with the same brutal determination he showed in life. Inscribed at the base of his statue are his words: Men, Do Your Duty.

www.ingramcontent.com/pod-product-compliance
Lightning Source LLC
LaVergne TN
LVHW011935070526
838202LV00054B/4662